BECOME A
U.S.
CITIZEN

DEBBIE M. SCHELL
RICHARD E. SCHELL
KURT A. WAGNER
ATTORNEYS AT LAW

SPHINX® PUBLISHING
AN IMPRINT OF SOURCEBOOKS, INC.®
NAPERVILLE, ILLINOIS
www.SphinxLegal.com

First Edition: 2007

Published by: Sphinx® Publishing, An Imprint of Sourcebooks, Inc.®

Naperville Office
P.O. Box 4410
Naperville, Illinois 60567-4410
630-961-3900
Fax: 630-961-2168
www.sourcebooks.com
www.SphinxLegal.com

This publication is designed to provide accurate and authoritative information in regard to the subject matter covered. It is sold with the understanding that the publisher is not engaged in rendering legal, accounting, or other professional service. If legal advice or other expert assistance is required, the services of a competent professional person should be sought.

From a Declaration of Principles Jointly Adopted by a Committee of the American Bar Association and a Committee of Publishers and Associations

This product is not a substitute for legal advice.

Disclaimer required by Texas statutes.

Library of Congress Cataloging-in-Publication Data

Schell, Debbie M.
  Become a U.S. citizen / by Debbie M. Schell, Richard E. Schell, and
Kurt A. Wagner.
    p. cm.
  Includes index.
  ISBN-13: 978-1-57248-597-6 (pbk. : alk. paper)
  ISBN-10: 1-57248-597-3 (pbk. : alk. paper)
  1. Naturalization--United States--Popular works. 2.
Citizenship--United States--Popular works. I. Schell, Richard E. II.
Wagner, Kurt A. III. Title.

KF4710.Z9S34 2007
342.7308'2--dc22
                2007008707

Printed and bound in the United States of America.
SB — 10 9 8 7 6 5 4 3 2 1

ACKNOWLEDGMENTS

The authors of this guide would not have completed this book without the generous contribution of time, support, and advice of many people. We would like to take this opportunity to thank the many individuals whose contributions are greatly appreciated. We wish to give great thanks to Andrea, Anna Lena, Nathan, and Christopher. We also wish to thank Bruni and Doreen for their unending support and substantial contributions.

Further, we would like to give a special thanks to Erin Shanahan and Lisa Findley at Sourcebooks for their patience and support for this project.

CONTENTS

INTRODUCTION: AN OVERVIEW OF U.S. CITIZENSHIP AND THE NATURALIZATION PROCESS

Why should I become a U.S. citizen?

What are the qualifications needed to become a U.S. citizen?

Can I become a U.S. citizen even if I do not have a green card?

How soon after getting my green card can I apply for citizenship?

Does my past behavior affect whether I can become a U.S. citizen?

If I marry a U.S. citizen, do I automatically become a U.S. citizen?

If my child is born outside the United States, is he or she still a U.S. citizen if I am a U.S. citizen?

This practical guide answers these questions, as well as many others on the issue of becoming a U.S. citizen. This guide also provides tips and suggestions for anyone who needs information, guidance, or the forms necessary to apply to become a U.S. citizen.

This guide focuses on acquiring citizenship through the process of *naturalization*. Naturalization is the route to citizenship used by lawful permanent residents (also called permanent residents or green card holders). Naturalization means that someone who was not born in the United States is eligible to become a U.S. citizen, and does so by going through the necessary steps and filing the appropriate paperwork required by the U.S. government.

Before you can apply for U.S. citizenship through naturalization, you must first have been a permanent resident for a period of time. In some cases, you must have been a permanent resident for at least five years before you can apply for citizenship, and in some situations you need only have been a permanent resident for three and a half years before you can apply for citizenship. Although it is not mandatory that a permanent resident alien becomes a citizen, many find that there benefits are bestowed upon U.S. citizens that they would like to enjoy. For example, U.S. citizens are allowed to vote in federal elections, apply for federal jobs, run for elected positions, and get U.S. passports.

Once you have decided that you would like to become a U.S. citizen, you must ensure that all of the eligibility requirements are met. In order to qualify for naturalization, you must satisfy several requirements, such as:
• residency;
• physical presence in the U.S.;
• appropriate age;
• good moral character;
• loyalty to the U.S. constitution;
• adequate English language ability; and,
• knowledge of U.S. history and government.

Once the basic requirements have been met, you are ready to start the process of actually applying for naturalization. The United States Citizenship and Immigration Service (USCIS) requires that certain forms, documents, and information be submitted when applying for naturalization. The required forms, documents, and information must be submitted in a particular order at particular times as instructed by USCIS rules and regulations. There are fees associated with applying for naturalization. These fees can vary depending on who the applicant is, the age of the applicant, and under which category the applicant is eligible to apply. USCIS also has specific rules on where your application for naturalization should be filed. This is usually determined by who the applicant is and where that person lives.

Submission of the naturalization application is not the end of the process. After your application package has been submitted and accepted, you will be scheduled to have your fingerprints taken and for an in-person interview with a USCIS officer. It is during this in-person interview that you will be asked about details of your application, your English language ability, your attachment to the U.S. Constitution, and knowledge about U.S. history and government.

If all goes well at the interview and your fingerprint results come back with no criminal issues that would bar you from becoming a U.S. citizen, your application for naturalization will be approved. However, there is still one more step to complete. After your application has been approved, you will be scheduled to participate in a swearing-in ceremony during which you will take an oath, sign paperwork, and receive your naturalization certificate, indicating that you are now a U.S. citizen.

Although this guide is thorough and contains much information necessary to navigate the naturalization process, it has been written so that you will be able to quickly and easily understand the eligibility requirements, the documentation requirements, and the necessary steps needed to complete the process. Abbreviations and acronyms have been avoided where possible so that the reader does not have to continually look up the names of organizations or agencies. This guide also contains various appendices that provide the most current and up-to-date information regarding relevant forms and websites. Finally, this guide contains sample forms and documents that are necessary for the naturalization application process.

However, one word of caution (and also a request for help) – Internet links are sometimes very short-lived. They may change without notice or simply disappear altogether. New links and new websites are being added every day. If you find a link that no longer exists or you find other sites that might be of interest and help to future readers of this book, please share them. We would appreciate hearing from you. Send your updates or suggestions to:

Law Offices of Kurt A. Wagner, PC
780 Lee Street
Suite 102
Des Plaines, IL 60016
wagner@wagneruslaw.com
schell@wagneruslaw.com
www.WagnerUSLaw.com

Debbie M. Schell
Richard E. Schell
Kurt A. Wagner

WARNING AND DISCLAIMER

CHAPTER 1: WHY BECOME A U.S. CITIZEN?

People become citizens for many different reasons. For some it is a lifelong goal because they are attracted to things available in the United States such as greater freedom or economic opportunity, or because they are attracted to the ideas expressed in the U.S. Declaration of Independence or Constitution. Others are influenced by the practical advantages of U.S. citizenship.

ADVANTAGES OF BECOMING A U.S. CITIZEN

For many individuals, U.S. immigration choices are driven by the desire to bring their families together. For example, permanent resident aliens can sponsor their spouses and children who are under age 21. Without a doubt, it is easier for a U.S. citizen to sponsor relatives than individuals in any other category. It is also much faster for a U.S. citizen to try to bring in a family member than it is for a permanent resident. A U.S. citizen may sponsor relatives, such as parents and siblings, while a permanent resident may not.

U.S. citizens also enjoy much greater freedom and ease in traveling to and from the United States. Although recent changes require U.S. citizens to travel with passports to Canada and Mexico, permanent residents have always had to supply more documentation when traveling. United States citizens may also remain outside of the U.S. for longer periods of time on business or personal trips. In fact, a U.S. citizen may live in another country and remain a citizen of the United States. A permanent resident alien who stays outside of the U.S. for too long risks losing his or her permanent residence status.

A U.S. citizen can also travel to places a resident alien may not be able to without first securing a visa. For example, permanent resident aliens may need what are known as *transit visas* if they need to travel through one country on their way to another country. However, a U.S. citizen might be able to travel through the same country on the way to another country by just using his or her U.S. passport. For example, suppose a permanent resident alien wanted to visit the United Kingdom, but he or she wanted to fly through and stay in Canada for a brief visit. Depending on his or her home country, Canada might require a visa to enter. A U.S. citizen would be able to travel to the United Kingdom and Canada with just his U.S. passport.

Although a national identification card requirement for U.S. citizens has been debated, there currently is no requirement that U.S. citizens carry proof of their citizenship with them. However, permanent residents are supposed to carry their green cards with them at all times. As a side note, permanent resident aliens should have a current card with them. This means they have the added task of making sure the card is renewed and up-to-date.

After 9/11, one of the key reasons that immigration lawyers have urged people to become citizens is that as a visitor or permanent resident alien, the possibility of being forced to leave the United States through deportation and removal always exists. Even though a person has lived in the United States for decades, owns a house, has a family, and pays taxes, he or she is always at risk for being deported for criminal activity or other immigration violations. A U.S. citizen in the same predicament might face a horrible scenario including one that involves spending time in prison; however, at the end of it, he or she would still be able to live in the United States. Although it is possible for a person who naturalizes to be stripped of his or her U.S. citizenship, this is rare. Unfortunately, the more common scenario is that a permanent resident can risk being deported for criminal acts in the United States.

Another reason that many immigration lawyers and activists have urged people to become citizens is that only U.S. citizens can vote or run for office. While it is true that only someone born in the U.S. may become the president or vice president of the United States, there are many other political offices that a naturalized citizen of the United States might be elected to. Naturalized citizens may also vote in any election that other citizens could vote in, assuming they are registered to vote and meet other state and local requirements.

Naturalized citizens may also be eligible to apply for a wide range of federal, state, and local government jobs—including ones that require security clearances. For example, many individuals working for the federal government as translators may find their ability to do classified work limited unless they are citizens of the United States. Sometimes the limits are purely economic. Permanent residents may find it difficult to obtain certain licenses and permits as well, including the ability to own firearms in the United States.

Two other benefits are also available to U.S. citizens. First, United States citizens use the U.S. citizen line at airports, which is often much faster, and U.S. citizens are able to use the U.S. citizen line at U.S. embassies and consulates. Second, in the event of an emergency or disaster that occurs abroad, the U.S. embassy will have the protection and evacuation of U.S. citizens as its first priority. As such, there is always the chance that a permanent resident alien caught in the same unfortunate event may not be able to obtain access to the same level of assistance.

U.S. citizens are also able to register for and use government programs. Citizens may receive financial assistance and other government benefits that may be difficult for permanent resident aliens to obtain. Also, one of the requirements for sponsoring people for entry into the U.S. is that the sponsor must agree to provide financial resources so the person does not become dependent on financial help from the federal or state government. In contrast, however, if the person was a citizen of the U.S. and fell on hard times, he or she would be eligible for financial assistance from federal, state, and local programs without any impact on his or her status.

DISADVANTAGES OF APPLYING FOR CITIZENSHIP

There are some risks to applying for U.S. citizenship. The biggest potential disadvantage to applying for U.S. citizenship is that by applying for naturalization, you give USCIS a reason to review your total immigration history. So, if you have done anything that leaves a negative imprint on your immigration status, then you are exposing yourself to serious risks, including deportation or removal from the United States. If you know of anything negative in your history or think there is even the possibility there could be anything negative in your immigration file, then you should talk to an immigration lawyer before filing for citizenship.

For example, if the applicant knows that his or her green card was obtained through fraud or lying during an interview, then he or she could be subject to serious penalties including deportation. If he or she lied directly or somehow misrepresented facts during the process and the USCIS found about it, then he or she would be subject to being removed or deported from the United States. There are numerous ways this could happen, such as if someone entered the United States based on stolen documents and used them to make a new identity. If this then came to light, the person could be deported because the USCIS should not have issued a green card in the first place.

Another scenario to be avoided is that any permanent resident alien who has voted in the United States should not apply for naturalization before consulting with an immigration attorney. Voting in the United States in an election as a permanent resident alien can have very serious immigration consequences.

The USCIS also reviews whether you have good moral character. Although there is no absolutely clear definition of good moral character, the USCIS is basically checking to make sure that you have not engaged in acts indicating bad moral character such as illegal gambling, prostitution, drug trafficking, or other similar acts.

Many people become U.S. citizens because they believe they will have greater opportunity for themselves and their family. Just as becoming a U.S. citizen may open some economic doors, it may also have some costs as well. If you want to become a U.S. citizen, you must take care of your tax issues with the U.S. government. In addition to that requirement, you should know that U.S. citizens are taxed on their worldwide income—not just money they make in the United States. This means that your decision to become a U.S. citizen may have significant tax implications for you. Anyone who believes they have tax issues should consult an immigration or tax attorney familiar with these issues.

The possibility of paying U.S. taxes on worldwide income is part of a greater issue involved in becoming a U.S. citizen – the role of dual citizenship. For years, the U.S. government tried to discourage people from retaining their citizenship in other countries. Now the government's position is less hostile. However, some countries do not allow their citizens to be citizens of another country.

Applicants should also think about the fact that U.S. citizenship may carry some very real risks of being a greater target in the world. After 9/11, the world has become a significantly less friendly place for U.S. travelers. Some travelers prefer to retain or acquire dual citizenship so they do not have to travel on their U.S. passports. This strategy may be effective for reducing risk, but it does expose the traveler to the possibility of greater scrutiny in entering the United States. Certainly, the traveler will need a U.S. passport to enter the United States. Depending on the country of dual citizenship, another country might offer less of a risk in international travel. At the very least, anyone traveling on a U.S. passport should be familiar with the risks and be advised of State Department warnings relating to the country he or she is traveling to. The U.S. Department of State issues travel advisories for different parts of the world, and it is wise to pay attention to them, because they can warn of political instability and the risks of violence against Americans.

Finally, one of the duties involved in being a citizen is the duty to serve in the armed forces during times of conflict. A male citizen of the U.S. who has dual citizenship is potentially at risk for serving in the armed forces of other countries, which could have serious immigration consequences.

Another point that should be emphasized again is that an application to naturalize is based on continuous lawful permanent residence. This means it is for permanent resident aliens in good status. Anyone who is already in removal proceedings may not naturalize. By filing for naturalization, you risk having the USCIS examine your entire immigration history, as well as the five-year period immediately before you file to become a U.S. citizen.

SUMMARY

Becoming a U.S. citizen is an important personal decision. Before filing for naturalization, a person should consider his or her current immigration status to be sure he or she is in good status as a lawful permanent resident. Then he or she should weigh the many advantages of greater security, opportunity, and ability to participate in life in the United States against the possible risks. For most people, there may be no or very little risk in having their entire immigration history reviewed, but for some it could end disastrously in removal proceedings. Naturalization is usually a relatively smooth process, but it can be a long and possibly expensive decision.

<u>Advantages of Applying for U.S. Citizenship</u>

• Achieve lifetime goal

• Greater freedom

• Security from deportation

• Voting rights

• Ability to hold office

• May be able to sponsor relatives or spouse faster

• Easier to travel than on a green card

• No more renewing green card

• Live where you want out of the United States for as long as you want

• Qualify for more government programs

• Better job opportunities with government

<u>Disadvantages of Applying for U.S. Citizenship</u>

• More scrutiny because you are contacting the USCIS

• Tax consequences may be severe

• Psychological cost of losing ties to home country and being part of the United States

• Risk of military service may be greater

CHAPTER 2:
WHO QUALIFIES FOR U.S. CITIZENSHIP?

Applicants must fulfill many requirements to become a citizen of the United States. Some requirements are a matter of passing a test and others are a matter of learning U.S. history and being sure that you can swear allegiance to the U.S. Constitution. Others requirements are a matter of time and residency. One of the most important requirements is that of being a permanent resident alien in lawful status.

PERMANENT RESIDENT ALIEN STATUS

A point that cannot be stressed enough is that a person must be in lawful status as a *permanent resident alien* in order to naturalize. This means that he or she must be a green card holder in good status. There are two tricky things to remember. First, the USCIS can look back over an applicant's entire immigration history when he or she applies to become a U.S. citizen. This means that even if he or she is currently in good immigration status, an applicant may still be subject to being removed or forced to leave the United States if a criminal offense or some other item with serious immigration consequences from the past is discovered. Second, even though there are physical residency requirements for both naturalization and for being a lawful permanent resident alien, the requirements to naturalize may be different from those of being a permanent resident alien. For example, to be in good standing in the United States as a lawful permanent resident, you must live in the United States, but to apply to naturalize in addition to living in the United States, you must also live in the USCIS district or state in which you plan to naturalize.

RESIDENCY REQUIREMENTS

Residency requirements for status as a lawful permanent resident alien and the requirements of residency related to naturalizing to become a U.S. citizen are closely tied together. Anyone seeking to naturalize must meet the residency requirement. There are several parts of this requirement, which can be very tricky. Unless you fall into certain exemptions, you must be able to show you have physically lived in the United States continuously for the five years before the application for naturalization. For example, a green card holder working and living in Canada would not able to meet this requirement unless he or she fit into some narrow exemptions.

PHYSICAL PRESENCE REQUIREMENT

You must have lived in the United States for at least five years before you file to naturalize. This means that you must have been physically present in the U.S. during that time. You should be able to show that you were physically in the U.S. with evidence of where you were living, which might include cancelled rent checks, paid utility bills, or mortgage payments on a house. In addition to showing that you lived in the U.S. during the five years prior to filing your application to naturalize, you must also be able to show that you were living in the state or the USCIS district in which you are filing your application for at least the three months immediately before you applied.

After you apply, you will also be required to show that you lived within the United States from the date you file until you are admitted to citizenship. The USCIS will only look at where you have been physically living. The laws that govern physical presence in the U.S. are very clear in their requirement that people planning on naturalization should be physically present in the United States.

In addition to staying in the United States before filing, a person hoping to naturalize must also stay in the United States after he or she files the application to naturalize. As lawful green card holders, they have to stay in the United States to remain in lawful status and not risk abandoning their permanent resident status. The same rules do not necessarily apply for counting time in the country in order to meet the naturalization requirements. As noted earlier, although applicants to naturalize must be lawful green card holders, they must pay attention to the different and simultaneous residency requirements.

If an applicant is going to be gone for a continuous period of between six months and one year, this could count as a period of absence from the United States. This could cause the applicant to lose his or her status as a permanent resident alien and also make him or her ineligible to apply for citizenship. It is very important that people who want to naturalize pay attention to the time before and during which they intend to apply to naturalize, because absences from the U.S. can have severe consequences.

Generally, applicants have to live in the United States before they apply to become naturalized. However, under the rules, applicants may be able to show they were living continuously in the United States despite an absence. These rules are somewhat different from the requirement that a lawful permanent resident alien live in the U.S. in order to preserve his or her green card status. Applicants must remember that the U.S. authorities can discover that the person was not living continuously in the United States, even if the applicant did not apply for or otherwise request a nonresident classification for tax purposes, did not document an abandonment of lawful permanent resident status, and is still considered a lawful permanent resident under immigration laws. However, the person applying for naturalization can try to show that he or she was living in the United States continuously by offering evidence of the following during his or her extended absence:

- the applicant kept his or her job in the United States;
- the applicant's immediate family remained in the United States;
- the applicant could still use his or her U.S. living space—it was not rented out; and,
- the applicant did not get a job or work in the country he or she was visiting.

People who plan to be gone longer than a year and hope to naturalize should consult an immigration attorney to structure a plan and be advised of the risks. It is important to remember that this period of time is only for the five-year period before applying to naturalize.

Applicants who are going to be absent for a year or more should consult an immigration attorney and file a Notice of Approval with the required fee. The application must be filed before the applicant has been absent from the United States for a continuous period of one year. Approvals under this form cover the spouse and dependent unmarried sons and daughters of the applicant who are residing abroad as members of the applicant's household during the period covered by the application.

The discussion above is for people who choose to leave the U.S. for some reason, but are not in the group of people who have left the U.S. with immigration issues that need to be addressed when they return. For example, if a lawful permanent resident leaves the U.S. and an issue aries when he or she returns, the person might be required to undergo a deferred inspection. In a deferred inspection, USCIS authorities admit the alien into the country, but then require him or her to come to a USCIS office to determine his or her status. If this goes well, the USCIS will admit him or her back into the U.S. The period of time between when he or she returned and when he or she was approved for readmission after a deferred inspection or exclusion would not affect his or her chances for naturalization like an absence would. An applicant who has undergone deferred inspection or an exclusion proceeding and is readmitted to the U.S. satisfies the residence and physical presence requirements just like any other application for naturalization.

> **PRACTICAL TIP**
> If you are filing the Notice of Approval, check that it lists the family members as covered.

Taxes

If a green card holder claims to be a nonresident alien to lower or avoid U.S. taxes, then he or she will also place his or her naturalization process in jeopardy because the U.S. government may determine that he or she has abandoned his or her lawful green card status. If anyone is trying to claim nonresident tax status to avoid paying U.S. taxes, this issue should be raised with an immigration attorney before filing, because the government may conclude the applicant has abandoned his or her lawful permanent resident status. If the U.S. government office denies the request, there is a process for appeal.

Spouses

Spouses may enjoy certain benefits as well, which means they may naturalize without meeting the continuous residence requirement. The person must be a permanent resident in good standing at the time of the interview and will have to meet the good character, English language, and civics knowledge requirements, and agree to support the U.S. Constitution. In certain cases, he or she will be able to avoid the residency requirements. In order for this to occur, the U.S. citizen spouse must fit into one of the following categories:
- be a member of the armed forces;
- work abroad under contract with the U.S. government;
- work as an employee of an American-owned firm or corporation that works to further foreign trade for the United States; or,
- be a priest or member of a religious order recognized by and that has a valid presence in the United States.

As mentioned earlier, U.S. law gives people in the military receive special consideration for naturalization purposes. While non-military applicants for naturalization must live in the U.S. for at least five years, the requirements for the military personnel are that the person applying must have served in the U.S. armed forces and have served for at least three years.

The applicant must also be a permanent resident alien. Applicants may also apply within six months of an honorable discharge if they are not applying while on active duty. Military personnel may also apply for naturalization without being lawful permanent resident aliens if they have served in the U.S. armed forces during what is known as a *period of recognized hostilities*. The current situation has been designated as a period of recognized hostilities by the President. This also applies for military personnel who have enlisted or reenlisted during the period of recognized hostilities. In case a military person does not fall within the special laws mentioned above, then he or she will have to follow the rules for applying to service centers, as would a non-military person.

In the case of students, an applicant who is attending an educational institution in a state or service district other than the applicant's home residence may apply for naturalization where that institution is located or in the state of the applicant's home residence if the applicant can establish that he or she is financially dependent upon his or her parents at the time that the application is filed and during the naturalization process.

A special class of alien are those who would live in the U.S. but commute across the border. Although they may be in the U.S. quite often, these aliens have to establish their residence in the United States, and they have to intend to live there permanently. That means they have to spend the required period of residence time before they can be eligible to naturalize.

If an alien moves from state to state as opposed to from county to county, then he or she should file in the state where he or she filed his or her annual federal income tax returns. If the alien changes residences for periods less than a year, then he or she should apply where he or she lived when he or she last left the U.S. to travel abroad.

Members of other organizations that are deemed to be in the national interest are also given a more generous interpretation of the rules. This accommodation applies to a wide-ranging group of entities, from relief organizations to banks. Anyone working for a U.S. company traveling abroad might want to investigate this option. People either working for the U.S. government or working for companies with contracts might benefit, as well as other U.S.-owned companies. For this exemption to apply, the person would have to have been physically present in the U.S. for an interrupted period of at least one year after being lawfully admitted for permanent residence. People who serve on U.S. ships should also consult immigration attorneys, because there are special rules for them as well. Finally, anyone who thinks the USCIS told them incorrectly they could leave and still be naturalized in error may also have options available not generally available to others.

If applicants leave the U.S. to perform functions for a religious organization, they have been absent only to do religious work, and their group has a bona fide organization in the U.S., they may be able to use this exemption. However, individuals will want to consult an immigration attorney to see if their group meets the requirements.

AGE REQUIREMENT

People who want to naturalize must be at least 18 years of age and alive. Military families are given more generous arrangements for naturalization that may allow naturalization after the person is dead, but this is rare. Congress also made some special provisions for victims of the 9/11 attacks. Although some options exist for special circumstances during war time and sometimes children can become citizens as part of another person's naturalization, in most cases, the person must be 18 or older.

Sometimes children become U.S. citizens automatically if certain conditions are met. Children born outside the United States and who live permanently in the United States automatically acquire citizenship if one parent of the child is a citizen of the United States, whether by birth or naturalization, as long as the child is under the age of 18 and the child is living in the United States in the legal and physical custody of the citizen parent. However, the parent must be a lawful permanent resident alien. This also applies to a child adopted by a U.S. citizen parent if the child satisfies the requirements applicable to adopted children. However, just as lawful permanent residents have to satisfy the physical requirements of living in the United States, so must children.

This scenario is different from children who are born in the United States and then plan to sponsor their parents who were not naturalized and who were not born in the United States. Children who become citizens because they were born in the United States may not sponsor their parents until they are over 18.

GOOD MORAL CHARACTER

People who want to naturalize must be able to show they have *good moral character*. They have to be able to show it during the time required by U.S. law, which is generally five years, and they have to show it during the application process and the period between the examination and the administration of the oath of allegiance.

Although the person applying for naturalization has to be able to show good moral character, the USCIS does the evaluation. The service is not limited to reviewing the applicant's conduct during the five years immediately preceding the filing of the application. In some cases, the USCIS may take into consideration an applicant's conduct and acts at any time before that period. The USCIS may also take into account the person's actions during the period after he or she applies and before he or she takes the oath to become a U.S. citizen.

One point applicants should be very aware of is that the U.S. government cares about crimes. Applicants must disclose any criminal act for which there was ever a formal charge, indictment, arrest, or conviction, whether committed in the United States or any other country. There is an exemption for purely political offenses, as there is in other naturalization matters.

In addition to these two very significant criminal barriers, there are some other obstacles to naturalization. The concept of crimes involving moral turpitude come up quite often in immigration matters. A *crime of moral turpitude* is a crime that involves doing something wrong that the person committing the crime should have known was wrong, such as stealing or robbing a bank. In the case of naturalization, if the applicant committed more than one crime involving moral turpitude, that person would be barred from naturalization.

Criminal Barrier Exemptions

United States immigration policy has some exceptions to criminal barriers to naturalization. There are exceptions for what are known as political offenses—crimes where the political nature of the crime outweighs the other parts of the crime. If the offense happened before the applicant was 18 years of age, there may be some exceptions available. Exceptions may also be available if that was the applicant's only crime of moral turpitude and everything including the crime and release from prison or jail all happened at least five years before the naturalization attempt is made.

These are exceptions for petty offenses. There is another exception that might apply if there is one crime of moral turpitude and the most the alien could be sentenced to was one year or less and if he or she only was sentenced to a term no more than six months. Anyone who contemplates needing one of these exceptions should consult an immigration attorney before applying.

Crimes Outside the United States

Another area of concern is if the crimes occurred outside of the United States. If the applicant committed two or more offenses, was convicted, and the total combined sentence that the court actually imposed on the applicant was for five years or more, and outside the United States, then the applicant would be barred. However, if it were a purely political offense as defined by the U.S. government, it would not be barring.

Sometimes the nature of the crime matters for naturalization purposes. For example, controlled substance crimes are treated differently from other crimes. Marijuana is treated fairly leniently in that if an applicant is convicted to a single offense of simple possession of thirty grams or less, then the applicant should be able to apply for naturalization.

False Statements

Under good moral character requirements, applicants must also avoid giving false testimony to obtain any immigration benefits. If the applicant made false statements under oath and intended to obtain an immigration benefit by doing so, this can be a bar to naturalization. This would apply regardless of whether the information provided in the false testimony would have made a difference in the person receiving the immigration benefit they were applying for.

Other Restrictions

There are certain specific bars to naturalization that also apply under good moral character. A person who is applying for naturalization should be very careful around these areas and consult an immigration attorney before applying because these areas can also allow the USCIS to remove the person from the United States. For example, a person may not be a habitual drunkard and naturalize, but they also may not be a permanent resident either. Trafficking in drugs is a barrier to naturalization and so is prostitution. Anyone who has committed or been found guilty of smuggling illegal aliens into the country will also be barred from naturalization. A person practicing polygamy has somewhat ambiguous status and should consult an attorney. People who make their money mostly from illegal gambling are also barred from naturalization.

There is a catch-all phrase in the laws that allows the USCIS to exclude people who fall within the general rules of moral turpitude. For example, there is a requirement that you must show you supported your dependents. Also, extramarital affairs may be evidence of moral turpitude issues. Time on probation may also come up. Although applicants may not be on probation when they apply, they may have been on probation or parole previously. An applicant who has been on probation, parole, or a suspended sentence during all or part of the period before naturalization can still establish good moral character. Likewise, a person who has received an executive pardon from the president or a governor before the period of good moral chartering begins may also establish good moral character.

Sometimes people with criminal issues related to immigration try to have their criminal matters expunged from their records. Having records expunged generally does not work in immigration matters where the goal is establishing good moral character. For example, in the case of drug offenses, USCIS may treat impingements as convictions. Also, an applicant who has committed or admits to committing two or more crimes involving moral turpitude during the time the USCIS looks at his or her moral character may not be able to establish good moral character, even though the conviction record of one such offense has been expunged.

LOYALTY TO U.S. CONSTITUTION

People who want to naturalize have to be committed to the principles of government for which the U.S. Constitution stands. This does not mean they have to approve of everything the government does or that they have to belong to a political party.

One of the requirements is that people who want to naturalize must be willing either to bear arms for the United States or to otherwise serve the country. Although a man might have reservations about serving in the U.S. military, men are expected to register for selective service if between the ages of 18 and 26. Conscientious objectors may still naturalize; however, they must register and affirm their loyalty to the United States.

If an alien does serve in the U.S. military, he or she has significant advantages when it comes to naturalization. However, if aliens become a part of the U.S. military, desert, and are court-martialed, then they may be barred from naturalization. Most people who try to get out of military service because they are not U.S. citizens may not naturalize, but there are exceptions to this rule for service during time of war.

The laws governing naturalization give U.S. military personnel different status for naturalization purposes. Military personnel have to serve in the U.S. armed forces for at least one year. Service in any branch will do, including a National Guard unit when it is designated as a reserve part of the U.S. military. These laws are for military personnel who are still part of the United States and who have served for at least a year. Applicants who believe they do not fit in those categories should seek the advice of an immigration attorney.

An example of the benefits of being in the military is that people applying under the rules governing the military do not pay fees. Applicants under this provision do not have to live in the United States for five years and they do not have to live in the USCIS district for three months. If a person will be deported or could be deported from the United States, then they may not be naturalized. However, military personnel may naturalize even if they could be deported, which is a huge advantage.

Some political positions have been determined by U.S. law to be incompatible with being a U.S. citizen. For example, people who are members of the Communist Party or who advocate overthrowing the U.S. government by force are not eligible to naturalize. Anyone who believes they may have an issue because of association with the Communist Party should seek out an immigration attorney because the requirements are very specific.

As part of demonstrating their loyalty, applicants for naturalization must take an oath of allegiance to the U.S. Constitution. If a person seeking naturalization is disabled or impaired, he or she can seek a waiver.

ENGLISH LANGUAGE REQUIREMENT

The expectation of the U.S. government is that people will naturalize and become citizens of the United States. As part of that process, the expectation is that they will participate fully in the civic life of the country, so there is a requirement that they be able to speak and understand English and that they understand the history and civics of the United States.

In order to be naturalized as a citizen of the United States, applicants must be able to demonstrate that they understand the English language. Applicants must be able to show that they have an ability to read, write, and speak words in ordinary usage in the English language. There is a test to determine whether someone has these reading and writing skills.

Applicants also must pass a test to demonstrate that they have a knowledge and understanding of the fundamentals of the history, principles, and form of government of the United States. There are exemptions from the test requirements for people who are unable — because of physical or developmental disability or mental impairment—to take the tests.

The English language requirement does not apply to anyone who, on the date of the filing of the application for naturalization, is over 50 years of age and have has been living in the United States for a period totaling at least twenty years as a lawful permanent resident alien. People who are over 55 years of age and have been living in the United States for periods totaling at least fifteen years before they apply as a lawful permanent resident are exempt from the English language test.

There are sample English-language questions to review in Appendix A. It is important to remember the test is oral (spoken), so if applicants do not understand or do not hear the question, they should ask for it to be repeated.

KNOWLEDGE OF CIVICS AND U.S. HISTORY

Applicants for citizenship must also have a working knowledge of U.S. history and civics. There is a sample list of questions included in the appendices. This section of the test is done orally and in English, so if the applicant has questions or does not understand the question, it can be helpful to ask to have it repeated. If the person filing is over 65 years of age and has been living in the United States for at least twenty years before filing as a lawful permanent resident alien, then he or she may be exempt from the civics/history test.

SUMMARY

Naturalization requirements are complex, and in some cases, only an immigration lawyer can tell what the rules will be. However, in most cases, if an applicant is at least 18 years old and no special circumstance apply, has been living in the United States for five years continuously (no departures of six months or more out of the United States), and is in valid status as permanent lawful resident alien, then he or she should be able to naturalize.

If the applicant has been married to and living with a U.S. citizen for the past three years, and the U.S. citizen has been a citizen for the past three years, then the applicant should be able to naturalize as well.

Military personnel who want to naturalize should pay close attention to whether or not they performed active duty during a time of war. Generally, if the applicant was in the armed forces for less than a year or discharged more than six months before he or she applies for citizenship, then he or she must have spent five years as a permanent resident alien. In the case of military applicants, if they spend time out of the United States on military service, that time does not count as time out of the United States. However, if the applicant was on active military duty during an authorized period of conflict within six months of applying or is on active military duty at the time he or she applies, then he or she may apply without having to be lawfully admitted as a permanent resident. Also, he or she may apply if he or she was physically present in the U.S. or in a qualifying territory.

In most cases, an applicant must also have spent three months in the state or district in which he or she will apply. This requirement is waived for military personnel on active duty.

Most applicants must spend the three-month period in the state or district where they apply. They must have continuous residence in the United States of five years. Applicants must have good moral character, knowledge of English and civics, and agree to support the U.S. Constitution.

In addition to the military exceptions, applicants who have served on U.S. ships or are the spouse of an American who has worked in certain American companies or research groups may be able to naturalize without living in the United States.

CHECKLIST

Applicants applying to naturalize should be able to answer "yes" to the following statements.

❏ I am at least 18 years old.

❏ I am a permanent resident alien (PRA) of the United States and I have a valid green card.

❏ I have been a PRA for at least five years.

❏ I lived continuously in the United States without any gaps of thirty months or more.

❏ I have lived in the district or state in which I am applying for the last three months.

❏ I can use English to read and write, and communicate orally at a basic level.

❏ I know or have learned the basics of U.S. history and how the U.S. government works.

❏ I am female OR I am a a male who has registered for selective service OR I am a male who did not register, but I have a letter explaining why I did not.

❏ I have not deserted from the U.S. armed forces and I have received an exemption.

PRACTICAL TIP
Applicants who have a criminal record or are concerned they are not valid green card holders (lawful permanent resident aliens) should not apply for naturalization before talking to an immigration attorney.

❏ I am willing to serve in the military or do nonmilitary service.

❏ I support the U.S. Constitution.

❏ I can and will take an oath of allegiance to the United States.

❏ If I do not fit into these categories, I have investigated exceptions:

   ❏ I am married to a U.S. citizen serving in the U.S. armed forces or qualifying international organization.

   ❏ I am a member of the U.S. military serving on active duty.

CHAPTER 3:
HOW DO I APPLY FOR CITIZENSHIP?

The process of applying for U.S. citizenship begins with a personal decision. You must first decide that you want to become a naturalized citizen. A permanent resident of the United States is not required to become a citizen. Chapter 1 of this book sets forth the advantages as well as some possible disadvantages of becoming a U.S. citizen and can help you make this important decision.

If you decide you want to become a citizen of the United States, there is another step you should take before actually applying. That step is to carefully consider whether you qualify. The naturalization process can be long and it costs money. It is not something you want to do if you know ahead of time that you cannot qualify. Chapter 2 of this book can help you decide whether or not you qualify. In most cases, the question of whether or not you qualify will be clear and easy to determine. However, if your personal situation or past actions are on the *borderline*—that is, they appear close to a disqualifying action—

do not give up right away. There are many exceptions to disqualifications, which will be discussed later.

Once you make the big decision and are reasonably sure you can qualify, the hard work begins. Applying for naturalization requires you to provide detailed information about yourself, your personal background, your family, your job, your education, and your travel. If you are the type of person who is well organized and saves all your important papers, the application process will be easier for you. If good recordkeeping is not one of the priorities in your life, you may find that you will need to contact government agencies, schools, family members, etc., to get the information you need to accurately complete the application. If your background is complicated by criminal activity, you may need to obtain official records, court decrees, etc., and seek the help of an attorney.

This chapter takes you through the application process in detail so that you can feel confident about completing the application form. This chapter includes information on problem areas and how to either avoid or address them; instructions on how to fill out each section of the application; tips on what documents to send with your application; and, details on where to file the application.

TIMING OF APPLICATION

Before you start to complete the application form, you will want to know when you can file it. The application for naturalization is not like a tax return or a visa extension request. There is no deadline by which you have to file it; you file it when you want to become a U.S. citizen. However, you must be eligible to file. This means you have met all the requirements to become a U.S. citizen before filing. So, the soonest you can file the application is when you meet all the requirements discussed in Chapter 2.

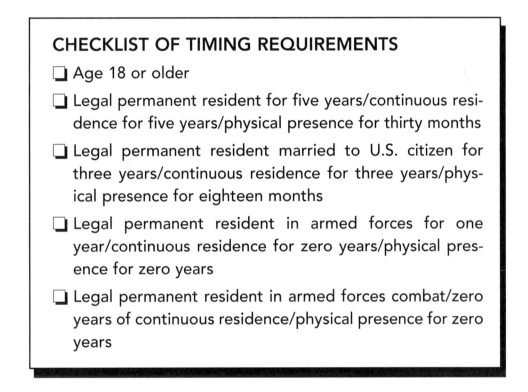

CHECKLIST OF TIMING REQUIREMENTS

❏ Age 18 or older

❏ Legal permanent resident for five years/continuous residence for five years/physical presence for thirty months

❏ Legal permanent resident married to U.S. citizen for three years/continuous residence for three years/physical presence for eighteen months

❏ Legal permanent resident in armed forces for one year/continuous residence for zero years/physical presence for zero years

❏ Legal permanent resident in armed forces combat/zero years of continuous residence/physical presence for zero years

CALCULATION OF TIME PERIODS

1. Date you obtained legal permanent residency: _____ (date on your green card)
2. Today's date: _____
3. Calculate the number of days between line 1 and line 2. This is the time period that you have been a permanent resident: _____

   (For example, the number of days from January 1, 2007, to December 31, 2007, is 365 because both January 1 and December 31 are included. If you need help in calculating the dates, many good Internet sites automatically calculate the number of days between two dates, such as **www.timeanddate.com/date/duration.htm**.)
4. Number of trips outside the United States for more than six months: _____
5. Total number of days spent outside of the United States since getting your green card on trips of six months or more: _____
6. Subtract line 5 from line 3: _____

   (This is the time period you have had continuous residence in the United States.)
7. Total number of days spent outside of the United States since getting your green card on ALL trips of one day (twenty-four hours) or longer: _____
8. Subtract line 7 from line 3: _____

   (This is the time period you have had physical presence in the United States.)

THE NECESSARY APPLICATION

The Application for Naturalization (USCIS Form N-400) is the only form you can use and the only form you need to apply for naturalization to U.S. citizenship. The form is available directly from the USCIS for free. The best place to get the form is on the USCIS website at **www.uscis.gov** (click on "Immigration Forms" at the top of the page). You can also call the USCIS Forms Request Line at 800-870-3676.

PRACTICAL TIP

You can apply for naturalization at the earliest ninety days before you meet the continuous residence requirement. In other words, if you need five years of continuous residence, you can send in your application for naturalization once you have continuous residence of five years minus ninety days. DO NOT send the application any earlier or it will be denied.

It is very important that you fill out this form completely and accurately. You are under oath when you fill out the form and if you supply false information, very unfortunate things can happen: you can be denied naturalization.

Form N-400 is divided into fourteen parts. Each part of the form is reviewed in the following sections, along with tips on what information to provide in each of the boxes of the form.

Part 1: Your Name

Enter your *A-number* (alien registration number) in the box at the top of the form AND in the box at the top of each page of Form N-400. The A-number was probably very important to you when you first

PRACTICAL TIP

It is also important that you know all the information that is provided on the form. This sounds easy because the form contains your personal information. However, if someone else fills out the application for you, make sure you have reviewed all the information on the form to ensure it is accurate. We once had a client come to us in tears because she was sent away from her immigration interview—someone else had filled out the form for her and had written down the wrong spelling of her name and the wrong address. When the interviewer asked her where she lived, she answered truthfully, but her address did not agree with the form. The interviewer became suspicious and sent her away to get additional proof of her actual residence.

acquired your green card, but with time you may have forgotten it. You can find your A-number on your green card, usually right in the middle of the card.

- Box A: Enter your current legal name in this box. This is the name on your birth certificate, unless you have changed it by marriage. If you are legally married, put your married name on this line.

- Box B: Enter your name as it appears on your permanent residence card (green card). Enter the name *exactly* as it appears on your green card, even if there is a mistake in your name on the green card.

- Box C: Enter other names you have used. Only enter names you have used in a public way (for example, if you ever used another name in a job or on a rental contract). Do not list nicknames that are used just by friends and family in social settings.

- Box D: As part of the naturalization process, you can legally change your name. You can become a new person with a new name and a new citizenship.

Part 2: Information about Your Eligibility (for Naturalization)

Check ONE of these boxes to indicate why you have the right to apply for naturalization. This could be five years of being a lawful permanent resident, three years of being a lawful permanent resident married to a U.S. citizen, OR serving in the military. The eligibility requirements are reviewed in the first part of this chapter and discussed in detail in Chapter 2.

> **PRACTICAL TIP**
> Think carefully before changing your name and about all the documents you may have to change or update if you change your name (driver's license, Social Security card, etc.).

Part 3: Information about You

- Box A: Enter your U.S. Social Security number if you have one. If you do not know your Social Security number, contact the Social Security Administration (**www.ssa.gov**). If you do not have a Social Security number, write "N/A" in this box.
- Box B: Enter your date of birth as it is on your birth certificate. Write the date in this order: month, day, year.
- Box C: Enter the date you became a permanent resident. You can find this date on your green card. Write the date in this order: month, day, year.

> **PRACTICAL TIP**
> Some immigrants may have acquired an individual taxpayer identification number (ITIN) because they were not eligible for a Social Security number. DO NOT enter the ITIN in this box.

- Box D: Enter the name of the country where you were born, even if the country no longer exists.
- Box E: Enter your country of nationality, even if it is the same as your country of birth. If you do not have a country of nationality because you are stateless, write in the name of the country where you were last a citizen or national. If you have dual citizenship, write in the name of the country that issued your latest passport.
- Box F: Check this box if one or both of your parents are U.S. citizens.
- Box G: Check the appropriate box to indicate your marital status.

PRACTICAL TIP:

If one or both of your parents are U.S. citizens, you should find out whether or not you are already a U.S. citizen before you complete and file Form N-400. Most of the time, if either of your parents is a U.S. citizen, you probably acquired U.S. citizenship at birth.

- Box H: Check this box if you are requesting a waiver of the English or civics tests.
- Box I: Check here if you will need any special accommodation during the naturalization process because of any disability you may have.

Part 4: Addresses and Telephone Numbers

- Box A: Enter your home address. Do not enter a post office box address— use a street address.
- Box B: Enter an "in care of" address only if you receive mail at a different address. If your home address and mailing address are the same, enter "same" in this box.
- Box C: Enter your telephone, fax, and email contact information.

Part 5: Information for Criminal Records Search

• Boxes A through G: Enter the personal data that best describes you. The information you enter here is used by the Federal Bureau of Investigation (FBI) together with your fingerprints to conduct a criminal background check on you. As discussed in Chapter 2, a criminal background can disqualify you for naturalization. However, you should know that the USCIS does not make the decision about your citizenship on the basis of your race, gender, age, or physical description.

Part 6: Information about Your Residence and Employment

• Boxes A and B: Enter in these boxes every place you lived and worked for the five years before filing your application. You have to enter all of the places you lived, no matter for how long and even if the residence was in a foreign country. You must also list all the places you worked, including periods of being self-employed or in

PRACTICAL TIP
Do not list the need for a language interpreter as a request for special accommodation. You are supposed to have a basic knowledge of English in order to qualify for naturalization. See Chapter 2 for more details.

PRACTICAL TIP
Be very accurate with the dates. Check to make sure there are no gaps in the dates of residency. If you lived in City A from January 1, 2006, to June 1, 2006, and then in City B, make certain that the City B's starting date is June 2, 2006. In these boxes, write the dates in the month, day, year format (i.e., 06/01/2006 is June 1, 2006).

PRACTICAL TIP
Many applicants find Part 7 one of the hardest sections to fill out accurately because most people do not ordinarily keep track of every trip they take. If you are not sure when and how often you were outside the United States in the last five years, start this section of the application by looking in your passport. Write down all the entrance and exit dates that you find. Use this list as the starting point for the list in Part 7. These dates are known to the USCIS, so you want to make certain that they are on your list. You must enter all trips outside the United States of twenty-four hours or more. These trips include trips to Canada, Mexico, and the Caribbean Islands.

the military service if that applies to you. If you were in school in the last five years, list the schools.

Part 7: Time Outside the United States

- Box A: Calculate the total days spent outside the United States in the last five years. Use a date calculator like the one at **www.timeanddate.com** if you need help.
- Box B: Enter the total number of trips outside the United States in the last five years.
- Box C: Use this table to enter all the trips you have taken outside the United States. Make sure you list the dates (use the month, day, year format) and the countries you visited.

Part 8: Information about Your Marital Status

If you have ever been married, no matter how briefly or where it was, you must complete this part.

- Box A: Indicate how many times you were married.
- Box B: Give details about your current husband or wife.

- Boxes C, D, and E: Answer these questions about your husband or wife.
- Box F: Provide details on any previous marriages.
- Box G: If your current husband or wife has been married before, give details about his or her previous marriages.

Part 9: Information about Your Children

- Box A: Enter the number of sons and daughters you have EVER had. This means you must list all your children, even if they are missing, dead, born in other countries, not living with you, born when you were not married, stepchildren, or adopted.
- Box B: For each child, enter the data required. If the child is missing, write "missing" in the current address box.

PRACTICAL TIP

Part 7 will often require an extra sheet of paper to enter all the trips you have taken. If you do add a sheet of paper to your application for this or any other answer, write the following at the top right hand corner of each sheet you attach: Your name, your A-number, the form number (in this case, N-400), and the part and box you are adding information to.

PRACTICAL TIP

Being married to the same person more than once counts as two marriages. Therefore, if you married your current husband or wife twenty years ago, divorced, and spent ten years single, and then married the same person again, you have two marriages.

PRACTICAL TIP

Part 9 can be a sensitive question for persons who may have had children when they were not married that they have not told their current husband or wife about. Nevertheless, the regulations are clear: you must list all your children. The application for naturalization is a private matter between you and the USCIS, but there are instances where spouses learn of the information provided on the form.

Part 10: Additional Questions

The questions that begin in Part 10 are used by the USCIS to see if you meet the eligibility requirements discussed in Chapter 2. The questions can make you uncomfortable and may be confusing. If any part of the question applies to you, you must answer "yes." For example, question 5 in part 10 asks, "Do you owe any federal, state, or local taxes that are overdue?" You must answer "yes" if you owe any ONE of these taxes.

If you are truly uncertain as to whether a particular question applies to your personal situation or activities, do not take a chance and just answer "no." Withholding information or answering falsely is a crime and can be used by the USCIS to deny your application based on bad moral character. Before taking a chance, consult a competent immigration attorney to find out how you should answer.

- Box A: Answer these questions "yes" or "no." For any "yes" answer, attach an explanation. The next section of this chapter includes tips on what documents you may need to supply to support any "yes" answers. Remember that answering "yes" to a question does not automatically mean your application will be denied.
- Box B: List all groups, organizations, associations, etc., that you have been a member of or associated with in ANY country.

Although answering "yes" does not automatically mean your application will be denied, if you answer "yes" to any of these questions, you will have to have a powerful and credible explanation to overcome a denial of citizenship. The prohibition against working with the Communist Party, terrorist organizations, and/or the former Nazi government are set forth specifically in the Immigration and Nationality Act, and unlike other prohibitions such as good moral character, much less interpretation by the USCIS is involved.

- Box C: Answer these questions "yes" or "no."
- Box D: Answer these questions "yes" or "no."
- Box E: Answer "yes" or "no" to these questions. You should know if any of these immigration actions apply to you.
- Box F: Answer these questions about your military service, if any.
- Box G: Answer these questions about selective service registration (sometimes called the *draft*) only if you are a male who has lived in the United States while you were between the ages 18 and 26.

PRACTICAL TIP
Being associated with an organization or association means being actively involved with it, supporting it, attending regular meetings, contributing money to, etc. It does not mean going to one lecture to learn about an organization or just being good friends with someone in an organization.

PRACTICAL TIP
Be particularly careful to answer "yes" and attach an explanation to any question where you had actual contact with the police or a court. Records of such contact often exist even if no arrest was made and even if the police say they will not keep a record of the incident.

- Box H: DO NOT COMPLETE THIS PART. These questions will be asked and answered at your interview.

> **PRACTICAL TIP**
> If you were living in the United States between the ages of 18 and 26 on a nonimmigrant visa (e.g., as a student on an F1 visa), these questions do not apply to you.

Part 11: Your Signature

Sign the application before you send it to the USCIS.

Part 12: Signature of Person Who Prepared the Application

If you did not prepare the application yourself, the person who prepared it must sign here. Even if the preparer is not an attorney, he or she must sign here and give the required information.

If an attorney prepares the form for you, he or she will also ask you to sign a Notice of Entry of Appearance as Attorney or Representative (USCIS Form G-28), which gives the attorney the right to represent you before the USCIS.

Part 13: Signature at Interview

DO NOT COMPLETE THIS PART. You will sign here after the interview. The interview process is described in the next chapter.

Part 14: Oath of Allegiance

DO NOT COMPLETE THIS PART. You will complete and sign this part at the interview. Your signature at the interview means that you have no objections to taking the oath of allegiance to the United States. You take the actual oath during the naturalization ceremony.

DOCUMENTS AND FEES

As you can already see, an application for U.S. citizenship is an exercise in paperwork. Form N-400 is complicated enough, but the application package can get even more complicated depending on your personal situation and your application status.

ALL applicants must send a copy of their permanent residence card (green card), two identical photographs with their A-number written in pencil on the back, and a check or money order for the fee.

The photograph requirements are:
- two standard, color passport photographs;
- printed on thin paper, unmounted;
- showing your full face from the front without any head covering (unless your religion requires you to wear a head covering);
- enough white space in the margin to allow you to sign the photograph if your application is approved; and,
- your A-number written lightly in pencil on the back.

> ### PRACTICAL TIP
> Now that you have completed your application for naturalization, do the following three things before you send it to the USCIS:
>
> 1. REVIEW all the information to make sure it is accurate;
>
> 2. MAKE A COPY of the application and all documents that you send to the USCIS; and,
>
> 3. KEEP this copy in a safe place so you can review the application before your interview.

The current fees involved in applying for naturalization are:

Filing fee for Form N-400:	$330.00
Biometric fee for fingerprints:	70.00
Total fees:	$400.00

You must pay the fee by check or money order drawn on a U.S. bank and payable to the Department of Homeland Security. Do not send cash.

PRACTICAL TIP

Always check the USCIS website at www.uscis.gov or call customer service at 800-375-5283 (TTY: 800-767-1833) to find out the current fee. One of our clients was quite upset when the USCIS returned a form that she had filed because the check she sent was $5 MORE than the required fee.

The other documents you need to send will depend on your answers to the questions on Form N-400. The checklist on page 46, adapted from the official document checklist provided by the USCIS, will help you decide what documents to send.

WHERE TO FILE YOUR APPLICATION

You should send your completed Form N-400 and all supporting documents to the USCIS service center that serves the area where you live.

If you live in Arizona, California, Hawaii, Nevada, the Territory of Guam, or the Commonwealth of the Northern Mariana Islands, send your application to:

USCIS California Service Center
P.O. Box 10400
Laguna Niguel, CA 92607-1040

If you live in Alaska, Colorado, Idaho, Illinois, Indiana, Iowa, Kansas, Michigan, Minnesota, Missouri, Montana, Nebraska, North Dakota, Ohio, Oregon, South Dakota, Utah, Washington, Wisconsin, or Wyoming, send your application to:

USCIS Nebraska Service Center
P.O. Box 87400
Lincoln, NE 68501-7400

If you live in Alabama, Arkansas, Florida, Georgia, Kentucky, Louisiana, Mississippi, New Mexico, North Carolina, Oklahoma, South Carolina, Tennessee, or Texas, send your application to:

USCIS Texas Service Center
P.O. Box 851204
Mesquite, TX 75185-1204

If you live in Connecticut, Delaware, District of Columbia, Maine, Maryland, Massachusetts, New Hampshire, New Jersey, New York, Pennsylvania, Rhode Island, Vermont, Virginia, West Virginia, Commonwealth of Puerto Rico, or the U.S. Virgin Islands, send your application to:

USCIS Vermont Service Center
75 Lower Welden Street
St. Albans, VT 05479-9400

If you live overseas and are filing Form N-400, you should send your application to the service center that serves the USCIS office where you want to be interviewed.

PRACTICAL TIP
This information can be found on the United States Citizenship and Immigration Services website at **www.uscis.gov**.

NATURALIZATION CHECKLIST

Step 1

Call the U.S. Citizenship and Immigration Services (USCIS) National Customer Service Center at 800-870-3676 to request the forms needed to apply for citizenship or visit their website at www.uscis.gov.

Step 2

Download the following forms from www.uscis.gov:

- N-400 (Application for Naturalization);
- N-426 (Military Service Certification), completed and certified by your Personnel Service Branch (military only); and,
- G-325B (Biographic Information) (military only).

You also need:

- Two each ¾" passport photographs, which can be obtained from any department store or specialty store that processes photographs;
- A photocopy of your resident alien card (green card) both front and back;
- A photocopy of your military ID card, both front and back (military only); and,
- A money order or cashier's check (current fee for nonmilitary is $330 plus $70, for a total of $400).

Step 3

Complete the entire N-400 application.

Complete side one of the N-426 and take to your Personnel Service Branch (PSB) to be certified (military only).

Complete the G-325B form (military only).

Place the following in an envelope and mail:

- Completed, signed and dated N-400 (Application for Naturalization) including all supporting documentation;
- Completed and certified N-426 (Request for Certification of Military or Naval Service) (military only);
- Completed G-325B (Biographic Information) (military only);
- Two each ¾" photographs;
- One money order for fee, made payable to Department of Homeland Security or U.S. Citizenship and Immigration Services (check with USCIS for current fees);
- Photocopy of your resident alien card (green card) both front and back; and,
- Photocopy of your military ID card, both front and back.

Step 5

Wait for the USCIS to tell you when you should have your fingerprints taken and then go to that appointment.

Helpful contact numbers:

USCIS customer service: 800-375-5283

USCIS Forms Request Line: 800-870-3676

USCIS website: www.uscis.gov

ALL FORMS CAN BE OBTAINED FREE OF CHARGE FROM THE USCIS.

CHAPTER 4:
WHAT HAPPENS ONCE MY APPLICATION HAS BEEN FILED?

Now that you have submitted a completed application for naturalization, there are still several steps that you must take. This process is truly a situation in which you have to be your own best advocate. That is to say, you must ensure that you are keeping track of your application as it winds its way through the USCIS.

This chapter explains what you should expect once the application package has been filed. Although the timelines may vary among different applicants and areas of the United States where the application may have been filed, the process is relatively the same everywhere. This chapter describes the normal procedure and gives you tips and information to help resolve problems if your application does not seem to be progressing according to USCIS timelines.

RECEIPT OF YOUR APPLICATION

On a daily basis, USCIS offices around the country receive an incredible number of applications from people seeking various immigration

PRACTICAL TIP

It is in your best interest to make sure anything you mail to a USCIS office is traceable either through the U.S. Post Office or through a private delivery service such as FedEx, UPS, or DHL. This is not the time to be frugal with mailing fees. It is absolutely worth your money to send your package either by receipt-requested mail through the post office or by a private delivery service that provides you with a tracking number and requires the recipient of the package to sign for it. Also, keep in mind that private delivery services will not accept packages addressed to a P.O. Box; therefore, if you are going to use a private delivery service instead of the post office, you must contact the USCIS or go to the website to get the correct street address for delivery.

benefits. The government is continually trying to improve its procedures for receiving and responding to the vast amount of paperwork it receives. That being said, it is still your responsibility to make sure that your application package is complete and filed with the correct USCIS office.

Once your package has been mailed and you have checked to see that it was received, you should mark your calendar for six weeks after that date. Within that time frame, you should have received a notice from the USCIS indicating that your package has been received and that your request is being processed. This information is printed on your Receipt Notice (USCIS Form I-797C) and contains very important information relevant to your application. The Receipt Notice indicates that the type of case you filed is the Application for Naturalization (USCIS Form N-400). The Receipt Notice also lists your name, address, A-number, and amount paid.

Other crucial information located on the Receipt Notice includes the receipt date, which is the date that the USCIS officially recognizes having received your application. Also, there is a priority date. This date is not relevant for naturalization applications but is very significant for various other types of applications that are filed with the USCIS.

The Receipt Notice will also have an application number listed on it. This is the number you can use to track the progress of your application within the USCIS system. If you need to contact the USCIS to discuss an issue with your case or to provide the USCIS with corrected or updated information, you will need to know this application number.

If you have not received any correspondence from the USCIS regarding your application within six weeks of when you mailed it, this could be an indication that something is not right. You should gather your files and make sure you have copies of your mailing receipt before you contact the USCIS to inquire about the status of your case. You will need to be prepared to provide the date that you mailed the application, the type of mailing service you used, and your A-number.

PRACTICAL TIP

If any of the information contained in the Receipt Notice is not correct, you must inform USCIS immediately so that the error can be corrected as soon as possible. Also, always be prepared to submit documentation to support your report that an error was made. For example, if the error is the wrong spelling of your name, provide a copy of your birth certificate. Likewise, if the error is an incorrect A-number, provide a copy of your green card showing the correct A-number.

PRACTICAL TIP

On the Receipt Notice there will be an estimation of time that USCIS predicts it will take before you are contacted for an interview. Often this estimate seems high (e.g., 565 days). However, do not set your calendar by this estimation! The time it takes to process an application often depends on how complete the application package is, how many officers are available to process such applications, and how long the backlog might be in any given office. These factors change on a daily basis. Therefore, applicants can often be pleasantly surprised by being contacted for their interview well before the estimated time. On the other hand, the processing of these applications can sometimes take longer than what was estimated. In such a case, you should be prepared to contact the USCIS about your case to make sure you are not being forgotten.

FINGERPRINTING PROCESS

Now that you have received your Receipt Notice, you can rest assured that your case has been entered into the USCIS system and is being processed. After you have received your Receipt Notice, you will next receive a notice indicating that you have been scheduled for fingerprinting. The notice will indicate the date, place, and time of your appointment.

Your fingerprinting appointment is usually scheduled at the biometrics facility located nearest the address you listed on your application. The notice for the fingerprinting appointment usually arrives a few weeks before the appointment to allow enough time to arrange your schedule so that you can keep the appointment.

However, the USCIS recognizes that sometimes emergencies come up. Therefore, if for some reason you cannot keep the fingerprinting appointment, you should contact the USCIS as soon as possible to request that the appointment be rescheduled. You can call the USCIS number located at the bottom of the form to make the request, but you should also follow the directions for rescheduling that are listed on the notice itself. The fingerprint appointment notice directs you to return the original notice with a written request that the appointment be rescheduled.

Although the fingerprint appointments are rescheduled quickly—usually within two months—you should not make any firm plans for when you think the new appointment date will be. You must wait for the new fingerprint notice to arrive before going to the biometrics center.

If you do not know that you have to reschedule the original appointment until the day of or very shortly before the appointment date, submit a letter with the original notice asking to reschedule. State that you are still interested in pursuing your application for naturalization and explain why you had to wait until the last minute to request that your appointment be rescheduled. If you simply do not show up for your fingerprint appointment and do not request that it be rescheduled, the USCIS will assume that you have abandoned your application and will stop processing your case. If this happens, you will lose any money and time that you have invested in the process up to this point.

When you go to the biometrics center, your fingerprints will be taken and then mailed to an FBI facility where a background check will be conducted. Remember, there are certain criminal activities for which you will be barred from gaining naturalization and for which you might be subjected to removal or deportation from the United States.

PRACTICAL TIP

If you have criminal issues in your background, it is advised that you seek the counsel of an attorney before submitting an application for naturalization to the USCIS. With the advice of an immigration attorney who practices immigration law as it relates to criminal law, you can make an informed decision about whether to file the application.

APPLICANT INTERVIEW

Now that your fingerprints have been taken, you will be notified of when your in-person interview will be. The USCIS will send you a notice that tells you when and where your interview will be. The notice also provides you with information about what you should bring with you to the interview.

Every applicant is required to bring his or her green card and valid passport. In some cases, the USCIS will request that an applicant bring additional documents to the interview. This request can be made because the USCIS file is incomplete or because requested documents were not initially submitted.

The USCIS will usually contact you just weeks before the scheduled interview, so plan to be in the country and available when the date arrives. Again, the USCIS recognizes that emergencies occur; however, it is in your best interest to attend the interview that you are scheduled for. If you have to reschedule your interview, there is no telling when your new date will be. It could be up to a year after the original date.

Once you have cleared your calendar for the interview and have gathered the documents requested in the notice, you should make final preparations for the exam. Make sure that you have studied the sample questions well enough that you are able to answer them. Likewise, be sure you have a good enough grasp on the English language so that you are able to speak and write an ordinary English sentence.

During the interview, you can expect the USCIS officer to ask you about the information you put on your N-400 application. The officer will be checking to make sure that the information that is coming out of your mouth is the same information that is on the application. If there are discrepancies in the information—for example, with dates or places—this might cause the officer to become suspicious.

The officer will ask you to speak and/or write a simple English sentence. The officer will also test you on your knowledge of American history and government. The officer can choose from a list of approximately one hundred questions. You are expected to answer six out of ten questions correctly. If you answer the first six questions correctly, the officer may conclude the test and move on with the rest of the interview. However, the officer may ask you all ten questions, even if you correctly answer the first six questions.

PRACTICAL TIP

There are some individuals who do not agree with the oath as it is written because of religious beliefs against war and/or violence. For such people, it is better to have raised this issue when you filed the application and not for the first time during the interview. The officer will ask you about your beliefs to determine whether they are sincere, but once satisfied, will be able to provide you with an alternate oath that takes into consideration your objection to the tenants of war and/or violence.

Once you have completed the verbal test on history and government, the officer will ask you to swear the oath that is printed on the last page of the N-400 application and ask that you sign your name to indicate that you have sworn the oath and that you agree with it.

At the conclusion of the interview, the USCIS officer may verbally inform you that you have successfully passed the interview and that you will soon get a letter to that effect in the mail. However, the officer is not obligated to tell you one way or the other whether you successfully passed the interview. In some cases, the officer will simply thank you for coming and inform you that you will get a letter in the mail indicating whether you passed the interview.

CHAPTER 5:
WHEN DO I FIND OUT WHETHER I AM A U.S. CITIZEN?

You will normally feel a great sense of relief after the interview, just because the whole process can be a bit nerve-wracking. If, at the end of the interview, the USCIS officer verbally informed you that your application was approved, you have reason to be happy. However, bear in mind that the decision is not official until you receive written confirmation of the decision.

APPROVAL OF APPLICATION

Soon after your interview, you will receive a letter in the mail officially confirming the fact that your application has been approved. At this point, you can be relatively secure in the knowledge that you have completed all but one step in the process of becoming a U.S. citizen.

Finally, soon after you receive the letter in the mail, you will receive yet another appointment notice (this should be the last one). This is for your swearing-in ceremony. The notice will contain the date, place, and time for your ceremony.

At the ceremony, you will likely be in a room with many other people – sometimes hundreds of others – who, like you, have had their applications approved and are now taking the final step to becoming a U.S. citizen.

During the ceremony, you will be required to surrender your green card. This is not a bad thing, since you no longer need it. You will also be required to swear the oath aloud in front of either a judge or other USCIS official.

At the end of the ceremony, you will then be given a formal piece of paper, which is your naturalization certificate. This document is very important and serves as evidence that you are now a U.S. citizen. With this document, you can apply for a U.S. passport, which will allow you to travel freely in and out of the United States.

In fact, it is highly recommended that you get your passport as soon as possible after you have been sworn in. There are usually one or more passport agencies conveniently located near swearing-in cites. It is not recommended that you keep your naturalization certificate on your person because there is a great risk of loss, and it can take up to one year to get a replacement certificate. Keeping your passport on your person as evidence of your citizenship status is preferred. Although losing your passport would be an inconvenience, at least it is be relatively easy to get a new one.

DENIAL OF THE APPLICATION

If you have properly completed Form N-400, submitted all supporting documentation, sent it to the proper office, paid the proper fee, and completed the interview, three things can happen:
1. your U.S. citizenship will be granted (the usual outcome);
2. your case will be continued because you failed the English or civics test or because you did not provide the proper documents; or,
3. your case will denied.

This part of the chapter deals with this last worst-case outcome. A denial can happen no matter how well prepared you are, but it is not the end of the line for you. There are more steps you can take.

Options for Appealing the Denial

The first thing to do if your application is denied is to stay calm. Then, carefully and completely review the denial notice. The USCIS is required to tell you why it denied your application.

Ask yourself whether the denial is based on a factual reason that you cannot deny or dispute. For example, if you were indeed an active member of a terrorist organization, you will find it next to impossible to overcome a denial made for this reason. More often, however, the denial is based on a fact that is not so clear-cut.

In reviewing denial decisions, the more common reasons for denials are lack of good moral character, lack of the necessary continuous residence in the United States, and tax reasons. These grounds for denial can sometimes be overcome through legal argument and the provision of additional documentation.

For example, a woman was denied U.S. citizenship because she was living with a man but not married to him. The USCIS examiner concluded that this was evidence of bad moral character. The woman was able to overcome this conclusion by showing that her living arrangement was as moral as any marriage except without a marriage certificate and that modern society accepted nonmarried partners living together as a morally correct arrangement.

The lesson to learn from this example is that if you think the denial was made incorrectly, you should try to appeal the decision.

To appeal a denial, you should start by filing a Request for a Hearing on a Decision in Naturalization Proceedings (USCIS Form N-336) with the office that gave you the unfavorable decision. *You must file this form within thirty days of the denial.* (You have thirty-three days if the decision was mailed to you.) To complete Form N-336, you simply indicate that you want to have a hearing and state the reason for the request.

You should prepare thoroughly for the hearing by addressing the specific reason for denial in detail. If you have not consulted an attorney up until this point in your application process, you should definitely do so in dealing with a denial.

If the USCIS denies your application after the hearing, you still have another chance to appeal the denial and try to get a positive decision. You can appeal the USCIS decision in a federal district court. This is a complicated and sometimes expensive procedure. You should consult an attorney before making a decision to take this step, in order to assess your chances of winning.

Reapplying for U.S. Citizenship

If your application is denied, you can sometimes reapply rather than fight the denial. Reapplying involves sending a completely new Form N-400 application, fees, etc. Reapplying is appropriate in the following situations:

- You were denied because you failed the English test and you now have improved your English.
- You were denied because you failed the civics test and you now have improved your knowledge. OR
- You were denied on another basis, but your situation has changed so that the situation no longer applies (e.g., you were denied because criminal charges were brought against you, but the criminal proceeding has now been decided in your favor, leaving you with no criminal record).

APPENDIX A:
QUESTIONS AND ANSWERS FOR NEW PILOT NATURALIZATION TEST

The following questions are compiled by the USCIS and can be found at **www.uscis.gov.**

If you are 65 years old or older and have been a legal permanent resident of the United States for 20 or more years, you may study just the questions that have been marked with an asterisk.

PILOT TEST QUESTIONS AND ANSWERS

AMERICAN GOVERNMENT
Principles of American Democracy

Q. Name one important idea found in the Declaration of Independence.

A. People are born with natural rights.

A. The power of government comes from the people.

A. The people can change their government if it hurts their natural rights.

A. All people are created equal.

*Q. What is the supreme law of the land?

A. The Constitution

Q. What does the Constitution do?

A. It sets up the government.

A. It protects basic rights of Americans.

Q. What does "We the People" mean in the Constitution?

A. The power of government comes from the people.

Q. What do we call changes to the Constitution?

A. Amendments

Q. What is an amendment?

A: It is a change to the Constitution.

Q. What do we call the first ten amendments to the Constitution?

A. The Bill of Rights

*Q. Name one right or freedom from the First Amendment.

A. Speech

A. Religion

A. Assembly

A. Press

A. Petition the government

Q. How many amendments does the Constitution have?

A. Twenty-seven (27)

Q. What did the Declaration of Independence do?

A. Announce the independence of the United States from Great Britain

A. Say that the U.S. is free from Great Britain

Q. What does freedom of religion mean?

A. You can practice any religion you want, or not practice at all.

Q. What type of economic system does the U.S. have?
A. Capitalist economy

A. Free market

A. Market economy

System of Government

Q. What are the three branches or parts of the government?
A. Executive, legislative, and judicial

A. Congress, the President, the courts

Q. Name one branch or part of the government.
A. Congress

A. Legislative

A. President

A. Executive

A. The courts

A. Judicial

Q. Who is in charge of the executive branch?
A. The President

Q. Who makes federal laws?
A. Congress

A. The Senate and House (of Representatives)

A. The (U.S. or national) legislature

Q. What are the two parts of the United States Congress?

A. The Senate and House (of Representatives)

Q. How many United States Senators are there?

A. 100

*Q. We elect a U.S. Senator for how many years?

A. Six (6)

*Q. Name your state's two U.S. Senators.

A. Answers will vary. (For District of Columbia residents and residents of U.S. territories, the answer is that D.C.—or the territory where the applicant lives—has no U.S. Senators.)

Q. How many U.S. Senators does each state have?

A. Two (2)

*Q. The House of Representatives has how many voting members?

A. 435

Q. We elect a U.S. Representative for how many years?

A. Two (2)

Q. Name your U.S. Representative.

A. Answers will vary. [Residents of territories with nonvoting delegates or resident commissioners may provide the name of that representative or commissioner. Also acceptable is any statement that the territory has no (voting) representatives in Congress.]

Q. Who does a U.S. Senator represent?

A. All people of the state

Q. Who does a U.S. Representative represent?

A. All people of the district

Q. What decides each state's number of U.S. Representatives?

A. The state's population

Q. How is each state's number of Representatives decided?

A. The state's population

*Q. Why do we have three branches of government?

A. So no branch is too powerful

Q. Name one example of checks and balances.

A. The President vetoes a bill.

A. Congress can confirm or not confirm a President's nomination.

A. Congress approves the President's budget.

A. The Supreme Court strikes down a law.

Q. We elect a President for how many years?

A. Four (4) years

Q. How old must a President be?

A. Thirty-five (35) or older

A. At least thirty-five (35)

Q. To become President of the United States, what must the person be at birth?

A. A citizen

Q. Who is the President now?

A. [Current president] (as of May 10, 2007, George W. Bush)

Q. What is the name of the President of the United States?

A. [Current president] (as of May 10, 2007, George W. Bush)

A. (President) George W. Bush

A. George Bush

A. Bush

Q. Who is the Vice President now?

A. [Current vice president] (as of May 10, 2007, Richard (Dick) Cheney)

A. Dick Cheney

A. Cheney

Q. What is the name of the Vice President of the United States?

A. [Current vice president] (as of May 10, 2007, Richard (Dick) Cheney)

A. Dick Cheney

A. Cheney

Q. If the President can no longer serve, who becomes President?

A. The Vice President

Q. Who becomes President if both the President and the Vice President can no longer serve?

A. The Speaker of the House

Q. Who is the Commander-in-Chief of the military?

A. The President

Q. How many full terms can a President serve?

A. Two (2)

Q. Who signs bills to become laws?

A. The President

Q. Who vetoes bills?

A. The President

Q. What is a veto?

A. The President refuses to sign a bill passed by Congress.

A. The President says no to a bill.

A. The President rejects a bill.

*Q. What does the President's Cabinet do?

A. Advises the President

Q. Name two Cabinet-level positions.

A. Secretary of Agriculture

A. Secretary of Commerce

A. Secretary of Defense

A. Secretary of Education

A. Secretary of Energy

A. Secretary of Health and Human Services

A. Secretary of Homeland Security

A. Secretary of Housing and Urban Development

A. Secretary of Interior

A. Secretary of State

A. Secretary of Transportation

A. Secretary of Treasury

A. Secretary of Veterans' Affairs

A. Attorney General

A. Secretary of Labor

Q. What Cabinet-level agency advises the President on foreign policy?

A. The State Department

*Q. What does the judicial branch do?

A. Reviews and explains laws

A. Resolves disputes between parties

A. Decides if a law goes against the Constitution

Q. Who confirms Supreme Court Justices?

A. The Senate

Q. Who is the Chief Justice of the United States?

A. John Roberts (John G. Roberts, Jr.)

Q. How many justices are on the Supreme Court?

A. Nine (9)

Q. Who nominates justices to the Supreme Court?

A. The President

Q. Name one thing only the federal government can do.

A. Print money

A. Declare war

A. Create an army

A. Make treaties

Q. What is one thing a state government can do?

A. Provide schooling and education

A. Provide protection (police)

A. Provide safety (fire departments)

A. Give a driver's license

A. Approve zoning and land use

Q. What does it mean that the U.S. Constitution is a constitution of limited powers?

A. The federal government has only the powers that the Constitution states that it has.

A. The states have all powers that the federal government does not.

Q. Who is the Governor of your state?

A. Answers will vary. [Residents of the District of Columbia and U.S. territories would answer that they do not have a state governor or that they do not live in a state. Mentioning the governor of the territory for Guam is acceptable. Any answer that mentions one of these facts is acceptable.]

Q. What is the capital (or capital city) of your state?

A. Answers will vary. [District of Columbia residents should ajswer that DC is not a state, and that therefore it does not have a capital. Any answer that mentions one of these facts is acceptable.]

Q. What are the two major political parties in the U.S. today?
A. Democrats and Republicans

Q. What is the highest court in the U.S.?
A. The United States Supreme Court

*Q. What is the majority political party in the House of Representatives now?
A. Democrats
A. Democratic Party

Q. What is the political party of the majority in the Senate now?
A. Democrats
A. Democratic Party

Q. What is the political party of the President now?
A. Republicans
A. Republican Party

Q. Who is the Speaker of the House of Representatives now?
A. Nancy Pelosi

*Q. Who is the Senate Majority Leader now?
A. Harry Reid

Q. In what month are general presidential elections held in the United States?

A. November

Q. When must all males register for the Selective Service?

A. At age 18

Q. Who is the Secretary of State now?

A. Condoleezza Rice

Q. Who is the Attorney General now?

A. Alberto Gonzales

*Q. Is the current President in his first or second term?

A. Second

Rule of Law

Q. What is self-government?

A. Powers come from the people.

A. Government responds to the people.

Q. Who governs the people in a self-governed country?

A. The people govern themselves.

A. The government elected by the people.

Q. What is the "rule of law"?

A. Everyone must obey the law.

A. Leaders must obey the law.

A. Government must obey the law.

Q. What are "inalienable rights"?

A. Individual rights that people are born with

Rights and Responsibilities

Q. There are four amendments to the Constitution about who can vote. Describe one of them.

A. Any citizen over 18 can vote.

A. A citizen of any race can vote.

A. Any male or female citizen can vote. (Women and men can vote.)

A. You don't have to pay to vote. (You don't have to pay a poll tax to vote.)

Q. Name one responsibility that is only for United States citizens.

A. Vote

A. Serve on a jury

Q. Name two rights that are only for United States citizens.

A. The right to apply for a federal job

A. The right to vote

A. The right to run for office

A. The right to carry a U.S. passport

Q. Name two rights of everyone living in the U.S.

A. Freedom of expression

A. Freedom of speech

A. Freedom of assembly

A. Freedom to petition the government

A. Freedom of worship

A. The right to bear arms

Q. What is the Pledge of Allegiance?

A. The promise of loyalty to the flag and the nation

Q. Name one promise you make when you say the Oath of Allegiance.

A. To give up loyalty to other countries (I give up loyalty to my [old][first][other] country.)

A. To defend the Constitution and laws of the United States

A. To obey the laws of the United States

A. To serve in the United States military if needed (To fight for the United States [if needed].)

A. To serve the nation if needed (To do important work for the United States [if needed].)

A. To be loyal to the United States

Q. Who can vote in the U.S. presidential elections?

A. All citizens 18 years of age and older

A. All registered citizens 18 years of age and older

Q. Name two ways that Americans can participate in their democracy.

A. Vote

A. Join a political party

A. Help out with a campaign

A. Join a civic group

A. Join a community group

A. Tell an elected official your opinion on an issue

A. Call your Senators and Representatives

A. Publicly support or oppose an issue or policy

A. Run for office

A. Write to a newspaper

Q. When is the last day you can send in federal income tax forms?

A. April 15

Q. Name two of the natural, or inalienable, rights in the Declaration of Independence.

A. Life

A. Liberty

A. The pursuit of happiness

AMERICAN HISTORY
Colonial and Independence

Q. Who wrote the Declaration of Independence?
A. Thomas Jefferson

Q. When was the Declaration of Independence adopted?
A. July 4, 1776

Q. Name one reason why the colonists came to America?
A. Freedom
A. Political liberty
A. Religious freedom
A. Economic opportunity
A. To practice their religion
A. To escape persecution

*Q. What happened at the Constitutional Convention?
A. The Constitution was written.
A. The Founding Fathers wrote the Constitution.

Q. Why did the colonists fight the British?
A. They had to pay high taxes but did not have any say about it. (Taxation without representation.)
A. The British army stayed in their houses. (boarding, quartering)
A. The British denied the colonists self-government.

Q. When was the Constitution drafted?
A. 1787

Q. There are 13 original states. Name three.
A. Connecticut, Delaware, Georgia, Maryland, Massachusetts, New Hampshire, New Jersey, New York, North Carolina, Pennsylvania, Rhode Island, South Carolina, and Virginia.

Q. What group of people was taken to America and sold as slaves?
A. Africans
A. People from Africa

Q. Who lived in America before the Europeans arrived?
A. The Native Americans
A. American Indians

*Q. Where did most of America's colonists come from before the Revolution?
A. Europe

Q. Why were the colonists upset with the British government?

A. Stamp Act

A. They had to pay high taxes but did not have any say about it. (Taxation without representation.)

A. The British army stayed in their houses. (boarding, quartering)

A. Intolerable Acts

Q. Name one thing Benjamin Franklin is famous for.

A. U.S. diplomat

A. Oldest member of the Constitutional Convention

A. First Postmaster General of the United States

A. Writer of "Poor Richard's Almanac"

Q. Who is called the "Father of Our Country"?

A. George Washington

Q. Who was the first President?

A. George Washington

*Q. Name one of the writers of the Federalist Papers.

A. James Madison

A. Alexander Hamilton

A. John Jay

A. Publius

Q. What group of essays supported passage of the U.S. Constitution?
A. The Federalist Papers

1800s

*Q. Name one war fought by the United States in the 1800s.
A. War of 1812, Mexican American War, Civil War, or Spanish-American War.

Q. What territory did the United States buy from France in 1803?
A. The Louisiana Territory
A. Louisiana

Q. What country sold the Louisiana Territory to the United States?
A. France

Q. In 1803, the United States bought a large amount of land from France. Where was that land?
A. West of the Mississippi
A. The Western U.S.
A. The Louisiana Territory

Q. Name one of the things that Abraham Lincoln did as President of the United States.

A. Saved (or preserved) the Union.

A. Freed the slaves

A. Led the U.S. during the Civil War.

*Q. Name the U.S. war between the North and the South.

A. The Civil War

Q. Name one problem that led to the Civil War.

A. Slavery

A. Economic reasons

A. States' rights

Q. What did the Emancipation Proclamation do?

A. Freed slaves in the Confederacy

A. Freed slaves in the Confederate states

A. Freed slaves in most Southern states

Q. What did the abolitionists try to end before the Civil War?

A. Slavery

Q. What did Susan B. Anthony do?

A. She fought for women's rights.

Recent American History and Other Important
Historical Information

Q. Name one war fought in the United States in the 1900s.
A. World War I, World War II, Korean War, Vietnam War, or Gulf (or Persian Gulf) War

Q. Who was President during World War I?
A. Woodrow Wilson

Q. The United States fought Japan, Germany, and Italy during which war?
A. World War II

Q. What was the main concern of the United States during the Cold War?
A. The spread of communism
A. The Soviet Union [USSR and Russia are also acceptable.]

Q. What major event happened on September 11, 2001, in the United States?
A. Terrorists attacked The United States.

Q. What international organization was established after World War II (WWII) to keep the world at peace?
A. The United Nations

Q. What alliance of North America and European countries was created during the Cold War?

A. NATO (North Atlantic Treaty Organization)

*Q. Who was President during the Great Depression and World War II?

A. Franklin Roosevelt

Q. Which U.S. World War II general later became President?

A. Dwight Eisenhower

Q. What did Martin Luther King, Jr. do?

A. He fought for civil rights.

A. He strove for (worked for, fought for) equality for all Americans.

Q. Martin Luther King, Jr. had a dream for America. What was his dream?

A. Equality for all Americans

A. Civil rights for all

Q. What movement tried to end racial discrimination?

A. The civil rights movement

Q. Name one of the major American Indian tribes in the United States.

A. Cherokee, Seminoles, Creek, Choctaw, Arawak, Iroquois, Shawnee, Mohegan, Chippewa, Huron, Oneida, Sioux, Cheyenne, Lakotas, Crows, Blackfeet, Teton, Navajo, Apaches, Pueblo, Hopi, Inuit [Adjudicators will be supplied with a complete list.]

INTEGRATED CIVICS
Geography

Q. Name one of the two longest rivers in the United States.

A. The Missouri River

A. The Mississippi River

Q. What ocean is on the west coast of the United States?

A. The Pacific Ocean

Q. What country is on the northern border of the United States?

A. Canada

Q. Where is the Grand Canyon?

A. Arizona

A. The Southwest

A. Along/on the Colorado River

Q. Where is the Statue of Liberty?

A. New York Harbor

A. Liberty Island

[Also acceptable are New Jersey, near New York City, and on the Hudson (River).]

Q. What country is on the southern border of the United States?

A. Mexico

Q. Name one large mountain range in the United States.

A. The Rocky Mountains

A. The Appalachians

A. The Sierra Nevada

A. The Cascades

Q. What is the tallest mountain in the United States?

A. Mt. McKinley

A. Denali

Q. Name one U.S. territory.

A. American Samoa

A. The Commonwealth of Northern Mariana Islands

A. Guam

A. Puerto Rico

A. U.S. Virgin Islands

Q. Name the state that is in the middle of the Pacific Ocean.
A. Hawaii

*Q. Name one state that borders Canada.
A. Alaska, Idaho, Maine, Michigan, Minnesota, Montana, New Hampshire, New York, North Dakota, Ohio, Pennsylvania, Vermont, or Washington

Q. Name one state that borders on Mexico.
A. Arizona, California, New Mexico, or Texas

Q. What is the capital of the U.S.?
A. Washington, D.C.

SYMBOLS

*Q. Why do we have 13 stripes on the flag?
A. Because there were 13 original colonies
A. Because the stripes represent the original colonies

Q. Why does the flag have 50 stars?
A. There is one star for each state.
A. Each star represents a state.
A. There are 50 states.

Q. What is the name of the National Anthem?
A. The "Star-Spangled Banner"

HOLIDAYS

Q. On the Fourth of July we celebrate independence from what country?
A. Great Britain

Q. When do we celebrate Independence Day?
A. July 4

Q. Name two national U.S. holidays.
A. New Year's Day

A. Martin Luther King Day

A. Presidents' Day

A. Memorial Day

A. Independence Day

A. Labor Day

A. Columbus Day

A. Veterans Day

A. Thanksgiving

A. Christmas

APPENDIX B:
PILOT NATURALIZATION TEST: VOCABULARY LIST FOR THE READING TEST

This list of words will help you study for the reading portion of the pilot naturalization test. When you take the test during your interview, you will be asked to read a sentence. An officer will give a sentence to you and you will read each word in that sentence.

You will not know the sentence the officer will ask you to read; however, the sentences will contain some of the words below. Practice reading these words. Keep practicing until you have learned to read all the words on the list.

PRACTICAL TIP
This information can be found on the United States Citizenship and Immigration Services website at **www.uscis.gov**.

Civics Vocabulary

1. America
2. bill
3. Bill of Rights
4. capital
5. city
6. Congress
7. Constitution
8. country
9. court
10. flag
11. law
12. laws
13. Mayflower
14. Pilgrims
15. President
16. right
17. state
18. states
19. First Lady
20. White House
21. Supreme Court
22. term
23. United Nations

Verbs

24. to be (is, are, was)
25. to be able to (can)
26. to come (come, comes, came)
27. to do (do, does)
28. to elect (elect, elects)
29. to have (have, has)
30. to help (help, helps, helped)
31. to live (live, lives)
32. to make (make, makes)
33. to meet (meet, meets)
34. to name (name, names)
35. to start (start, starts)
36. to veto (veto, vetoes)
37. to vote (vote, votes)

People

38. Abraham Lincoln
39. George Washington
40. Martin Luther King, Jr.

Holidays

41. Columbus Day
42. Fourth of July
43. Independence Day
44. Labor Day
45. Memorial Day
46. Presidents' Day
47. Thanksgiving
48. Veterans' Day

Places

49. United Nations' Building
50. United States

Other Words

51. a
52. color
53. colors
54. father
55. for
56. here
57. highest
58. how many
59. in
60. largest
61. most
62. new
63. of
64. one
65. or
66. our
67. people
68. the
69. we
70. what
71. when
72. where
73. which
74. who
75. red
76. September
77. speech
78. supreme
79. white
80. wife

APPENDIX C: PILOT NATURALIZATION TEST: VOCABULARY LIST FOR THE WRITING TEST

The list of words below will help you study for the written portion of the pilot naturalization test. When you take the test during your interview, you will be asked to write a sentence. An officer will read a sentence to you and you will write down everything that the officer reads. Listen very carefully and write down every word clearly.

PRACTICAL TIP
This information can be found on the United States Citizenship and Immigration Services website at **www.uscis.gov**.

You will not know the sentence the officer will ask you to write; however, the sentences will contain some of the words below. Practice writing these words. Ask someone to read each word to you and write it down. Keep practicing until you have learned to write all the words on the list.

Civics Vocabulary

1. American Indians
2. bill
3. capital
4. civil
5. Civil War
6. Congress
7. Constitution
8. country
9. First Lady
10. flag
11. freedom
12. law
13. laws
14. Mayflower
15. Pilgrims
16. President
17. right
18. rights
19. state
20. states
21. Supreme Court
22. term
23. United Nations

Verbs

24. to be (is, are, was)
25. to be able to (can)
26. to elect (elect, elects)
27. to have (have, has)
28. to help (help, helps, helped)
29. to live (live, lives)
30. to make (make, makes)
31. to meet (meet, meets)
32. to start (start, starts)
33. to veto (veto, vetoes)
34. to vote (vote, votes)

People

35. Abraham Lincoln
36. George Washington

Holidays

37. Columbus Day
38. Fourth of July or 4th of July
39. Independence Day
40. Labor Day
41. Memorial Day
42. Presidents' Day
43. Thanksgiving
44. Veterans' Day

Places

45. Alaska
46. California
47. New York
48. New York City
49. The United States
50. Washington, D.C.

Other Words

51. a
52. and
53. blue
54. building
55. court
56. during
57. father
58. February
59. fifty
60. first
61. for
62. he
63. highest
64. house
65. in
66. January
67. July
68. land
69. largest
70. leader
71. May
72. most
73. new
74. November
75. October
76. of
77. on
78. one

79. our
80. people
81. press
82. red
83. September
84. speech
85. supreme
86. the
87. we
88. white
89. wife

APPENDIX D:
LEARN ABOUT THE UNITED STATES: QUICK CIVICS LESSONS

The information located in this appendix is also located at **www.uscis.gov**.

To become a United States citizen, you need to learn about the history of the United States and how its government works. Knowing about your new country is a very important part of being a good citizen.

Quick Civics Lessons will help you learn more about U.S. history and government as you prepare for citizenship. This booklet provides short lessons, based on each of the sample civics questions that you should study for your naturalization test. As you study the questions and answers, you can learn more about the topic by reading the paragraph. To help you learn words that may not be familiar, a glossary is provided at the end.

The United States has a rich, interesting history and a unique system of government. Learning more about the United States as you

naturalize will help make your journey toward U.S. citi-
ship more meaningful. During your naturalization interview, you
will not be tested on the additional information in the short lessons.

The USCIS Civics Flashcards are a useful study tool for those preparing
to take the naturalization test. These colorful, easy-to-use cards present
each of the questions that can be asked during the test. The Civics
Flashcards are available for free online at **www.uscis.gov/graphics/
citizenship**. Hard copies can be ordered from the Government Printing
Office (GPO) by calling 866-512-1800 or by going online to
http://bookstore.gpo.gov and searching for "flashcards."

Q. Why did the Pilgrims come to America?

A. To gain religious freedom
In the early 1600s, the Pilgrims left England. They first went to
Holland, where they lived for a few years before coming to
America. Many English settlers sailed across the Atlantic Ocean
to the American colonies during the seventeenth century. Many
came for political freedom or, like the Pilgrims, the right to practice their religion. Others came because of economic opportunity.
These freedoms and opportunities often did not exist in the home
countries of these settlers. For them, the American colonies meant
a new chance in life and the freedom to live as they wanted.

Q. What is the name of the ship that brought the Pilgrims to America?

A. The Mayflower
The Mayflower left from Plymouth, England, on September 6,
1620. After sixty-five days crossing the ocean, the ship landed in

what is now the state of Massachusetts. Soon after, the Pilgrims signed an agreement called the Mayflower Compact. In it, the Pilgrims agreed to unite into a "Civil Body Politic." The Compact did not set up a governing system, as the Constitution later would. It did, however, contain the idea that the people freely agreed to live under the government. The power of this government came directly from the people themselves.

Q. Who helped the Pilgrims in America?

A. The American Indians/Native Americans

At the time of the Pilgrims' arrival, great Indian tribes such as the Navajo, Sioux, Cherokee, and Seminoles lived in America. When the Pilgrims came to America, they settled in an area where a tribe called the Wampanoag lived. The Wampanoag taught the Pilgrims important skills, such as how to grow corn, beans, and squash. As more Europeans moved to America, relations with the Indians were not always peaceful. Eventually, after much bloodshed, the settlers defeated the Indian tribes and took much of their land.

Q. What holiday was celebrated for the first time by American colonists?

A. Thanksgiving

The first Thanksgiving feast was held in Massachusetts in 1621. The Pilgrims gave thanks for a successful fall harvest. They learned from local Native Americans, or Indians, which crops would grow and how best to grow them. The Indians' lessons helped the Pilgrims grow enough food to survive the winter. In 1941, President Franklin D. Roosevelt signed a bill that officially made the last Thursday of November Thanksgiving Day.

Q. What do we celebrate on the 4th of July?

A. Independence Day

On July 2, 1776, Congress voted for the United States to become independent from Great Britain. However, we celebrate Independence Day on July 4. This is because it took two days for Congress to vote to accept the official Declaration of Independence. This Declaration was written by Thomas Jefferson and edited by Congress. It explained why the American colonies were separating from their British ruler. The 4th of July is now considered to be the birthday of America. We celebrate with parades, fireworks, the playing of patriotic songs, and live readings of the Declaration of Independence.

Q. Independence Day celebrates independence from whom?

A. Great Britain

The decision to break from the British was not an easy choice for many colonists. However, Great Britain's "repeated injuries" against the Americans, as noted in the Declaration of Independence, convinced many to join the rebellion. After years of difficult fighting, the colonists won their freedom.

Q. What country did we fight during the Revolutionary War?

A. Great Britain

The American colonists' anger had been building for years before the Revolutionary War began. The Americans fought the war because they wanted freedom from British rule. The fighting of the war ended in 1781, after the Battle of Yorktown. The

Americans won this battle with France's help. It was not until 1783, though, that the British fully accepted the United States' independence.

Q. Who said, "Give me liberty or give me death"?

A. Patrick Henry

Patrick Henry was a fiery leader of the American Revolution. Before U.S. independence, he spoke out for colonial rights within the Virginia legislature. Henry represented Virginia in both the First and Second Continental Congresses. He helped push the colonies toward independence. In 1775, when the Revolutionary War began, Henry convinced Virginia to join the colonists' side. Later he became the first governor of Virginia.

Q. Who was the main writer of the Declaration of Independence?

A. Thomas Jefferson

Jefferson was a Virginia lawyer and planter when he wrote the Declaration in 1776. He would become a very important political leader and thinker. Before becoming President, he was the governor of Virginia and the first U.S. Secretary of State. Jefferson strongly supported individual rights, especially freedom of religion. Because he wanted to protect these rights, Jefferson opposed a strong national government. Instead, he argued for states' rights. He wanted America to be a nation of small farmers who actively participated in their democracy.

Q. When was the Declaration of Independence adopted?

A. July 4, 1776

In 1774, representatives from twelve of the colonies met in Philadelphia, for the First Continental Congress. They protested British laws that treated them unfairly. They also began to organize an army. After fighting started between the colonists and the British army, a Second Continental Congress met. This group appointed Jefferson and others to create the Declaration of Independence. This document stated that if a government does not protect the rights of the people then the people can create a new government. Following this idea, the colonists broke from their British rulers and formed a new country.

Q. What are some of the basic beliefs of the Declaration of Independence?

A. That all men are created equal and have the right to life, liberty, and the pursuit of happiness

The Declaration of Independence is based on ideas about freedom and individual rights. Jefferson and the founding fathers believed that people are born with natural rights that no government can take away. Government exists only to protect these rights. Because the people voluntarily give up power to a government, they can take that power back. The British government was not protecting the rights of the colonists, so they took back their power and separated from Great Britain.

Q. What is the national anthem of the United States?

A. The Star-Spangled Banner

During the War of 1812, British soldiers invaded the United States. On the night of September 13, 1814, British warships bombed Fort McHenry. This fort protected the city of Baltimore.

An American named Francis Scott Key watched the fierce bombing and thought that the fort would fall. As the sun rose the next morning, Key looked toward the fort. He saw that the American flag above the fort was still flying, proving that the United States had not been defeated. Key immediately wrote the words to "The Star-Spangled Banner."

Q. Who wrote The Star-Spangled Banner?

A. Francis Scott Key

Key first wrote the words to "The Star-Spangled Banner" as a poem. He named this poem "The Defence of Fort M'Henry." Many years later music was added to the words of the poem. This music came from a piece called "Anacreon in Heaven." The combination of the poem with the music created the song that is now so well-known. It was not until 1931, that Congress passed a law naming "The Star-Spangled Banner" the official national anthem.

Q. What are the colors of our flag?

A. Red, white, and blue

We call the American flag the "Stars and Stripes." Congress chose the "Stars and Stripes" design for our flag on June 14, 1777. Americans celebrate June 14th as Flag Day. Much later, Congress explained the colors – red stands for hardiness and valor, white for purity and inno-cence, and blue for vigilance, perseverance, and justice.

Q. How many stars are there on our flag?

A. There are fifty stars on our flag.

Each star represents a state. This is why the number of stars has changed over the years from thirteen to fifty. The number of stars reached fifty in 1959. In that year, Hawaii joined the United States as the fiftieth state.

Q. What do the stars on the flag mean?

A. Each star represents one state.

The white stars on the flag represent the United States as being like "a new constellation" in the sky. The nation was seen as a new constellation because the republican system of government was new and different in the 1770s. Very few other countries were republics at that time. In the republican system of government, leaders work to help all of the country's people. They do not act to help only a few special citizens. Since the people themselves choose these leaders, the people hold the power of government.

Q. What color are the stars on our flag?

A. The stars on our flag are white.

The stars represent the founding fathers' view of the American experiment in democracy. To them, the goal of a republic based on individual freedom was a noble, lofty idea. Stars are considered a symbol of the heavens and the high, ambitious goal that our founders were trying to reach.

Q. How many stripes are there on our flag?

A. There are thirteen stripes on our flag.

For eighteen years after becoming an independent country, the United States had only thirteen states. In 1794, Kentucky and Vermont joined the United States, making the number of states fifteen. At that time, Congress increased the number of stars and stripes on the flag from thirteen to fifteen. The number of stripes was not changed back to thirteen for many years.

Q. What do the stripes on the flag represent?

A. The first thirteen states.

In 1818, Congress decided that the number of stripes on the flag should always be thirteen. This would honor the original states, no matter how many new states would join the United States later. These original thirteen states had been colonies of Great Britain before America's independence.

Q. What colors are the stripes on the flag?

A. The stripes on the flag are red and white.

The pre-independence American flags also had stripes. The "Boston Liberty" flag, for example, was flown in the early part of the American Revolution. This flag was flown by a famous group of patriots called the Sons of Liberty. This group and others felt that British laws treated the American colonists unfairly. They were angry about being taxed by the British while having no or representation in the government.

Q. What were the thirteen original states of the United States called before they were states?

A. Colonies

European countries began taking control of areas of America in the 1500s. These European-controlled areas were called colonies. England's first successful American colony was Virginia. Virginia began in 1607, as a small camp at Jamestown. Later, Pennsylvania was founded as a home for a religious group, the Quakers. This group opposed war and rejected all rituals and oaths. The Dutch colony of New Netherlands was captured by British forces in 1664, and renamed New York. The thirteen American colonies would later unite into one country, but the history of each one was quite distinct.

Q. What were the original thirteen states?

A. Virginia, Massachusetts, Maryland, Rhode Island, Connecticut, New Hampshire, North Carolina, South Carolina, New York, New Jersey, Pennsylvania, Delaware, and Georgia

These thirteen states were colonies before the United States became an independent country. The British king ruled the thirteen colonies, but Great Britain was very far away and focused on domestic affairs and wars in Europe, instead of focusing on the colonies. This meant that, even before their independence, the colonies largely governed themselves. This was done partly through colonial legislatures. These legislatures were elected by the colonists. Until the American Revolution, though, most colonists considered the British king their true ruler.

Q. What is the Constitution?

A. The supreme law of the United States

The U.S. Constitution has been in place longer than any other country's constitution. It is the basic legal framework establishing the U.S. government. Every person, agency, and department of government must follow the Constitution. This is why it is called the "supreme law of the land." Under this system, the powers of the national government are limited to those written in the Constitution. The guiding principle behind this system is often called the rule of law.

Q. What is the supreme law of the United States?

A. The Constitution

The government set up by the Constitution is based on the consent, or agreement, of the governed. The introduction to the Constitution reflects this idea. This introduction is called the Preamble. It states that "we the People" establish the Constitution. The actual system of the U.S. government is a representative democracy. The Constitution also reflects the idea of consent of the governed. The "governed" – all U.S. citizens – choose representatives to make the nation's laws and a president to lead the executive branch.

Q. In what year was the Constitution written?

A. 1787

Before the U.S. Constitution, the Articles of Confederation was the document that established the U.S. system of government. The Articles were ratified in 1783. By 1786, many American leaders had become unhappy with this document. The national government it set up was too weak. In 1787, Congress decided that a convention would meet in Philadelphia to revise the Articles. At this meeting, the leaders quickly decided to go beyond revising the Articles. Instead, they wrote a whole new governing document – the Constitution.

Q. What is the introduction to the Constitution called?

A. The Preamble

The preamble says: "We the People of the United States, in Order to form a more perfect Union, establish Justice, insure domestic Tranquility, provide for the common defense, promote the general Welfare, and secure the Blessings of Liberty to ourselves and our

Posterity, do ordain and establish this Constitution for the United States of America." This means that our government was set up by the people, so that it would be responsive to them and protect their rights. All power to govern comes from the people, who hold the highest power. This idea is known as popular sovereignty.

Q. What kind of government does the United States have?

A. A Republic

In a republic, the power that the government exercises comes from the people themselves. The government is responsible for protecting the rights of all persons, not just a few special people. The way this happens in the United States is through a system of representative democracy. The people freely choose who will lead them and represent their interests. President Abraham Lincoln said our republican government is "of the people, by the people, and for the people."

Q. What are the two major political parties in the United States today?

A. The Democratic and Republican parties

The Constitution did not establish political parties, and George Washington specifically warned against them. Still, a split between two political groups, the Democratic-Republicans and the Federalists, appeared early in U.S. history. The current Democratic Party was created from the old Democratic-Republicans by President Andrew Jackson. The Republican Party took over from the Whigs as a major party in the 1860s. Abraham Lincoln, who was first elected in 1860, was the first Republican

President. Throughout U.S. history, other parties, such as the Know-Nothing, Bull-Moose (also called Progressive), Reform, and Green Parties, have played various roles in American politics.

Q. How many branches are there in the United States government?

A. Three

The writers of the Constitution believed that no single group in the government should have total power. They thought that any person or group that had total power over the government would abuse it. In creating the U.S. system, they followed the idea of separation of powers. Along with checks and balances between the different parts of the government, the separation of powers into three branches prevents the concentration of power. This means that the rights of citizens are better protected. The powers to make laws, to execute laws, and to interpret the laws are given to different branches.

Q. What are the three branches of our government?

A. Executive, Judicial, and Legislative

The Constitution divides the government's power among three branches. These branches operate under a system of checks and balances. This means that each branch can potentially block the action of another branch. This means that no single branch can grow too powerful and harm the liberties of citizens. For example, the Senate can block a treaty signed by the President, or the U.S. Supreme Court can reject a law passed by Congress. In the first example, the legislative branch is "checking" the executive branch, and in the second, the judicial branch is "checking" the legislative branch.

Q. What is the executive branch of our government?

A. The President, the Cabinet, and departments under the cabinet members

The job of the executive branch is to carry out, or execute, the laws of the nation. While the Constitution does discuss the Cabinet, it does not say what each federal department or agency should do. Throughout U.S. history, Congress has established the specific functions of these organizations. The State Department, Department of Homeland Security, and Environmental Protection Agency are three examples of federal departments.

Q. Who is the head of the executive branch of the U.S. Government?

The President

The President is both the head of state and the head of government. Presidential powers include the ability to sign treaties with other countries and select ambassadors to represent the United States abroad. As head of the executive branch, the President names the top leaders of the federal departments. However, the Senate has the power to reject the President's choices. This limit on the power of the President is another example of checks and balances.

Q. What are some of the requirements to be eligible to become President?

A. A candidate for President must: be a native-born citizen, be at least thirty-five years old, and have lived in the U.S. for at least fourteen years.

The writers of the Constitution wanted the President to be an experienced leader with a strong connection to the United States.

The eligibility requirements try to make sure that this happens. In Federalist Paper #64, John Jay wrote that the President should be a man "of whom the people have had time to form a judgment." This, Jay explains, is one main reason for the eligibility requirements. The youngest person in American history to become President was Theodore Roosevelt. Roosevelt entered the White House when he was forty-two years old.

Q. Who elects the President of the United States?

A. The Electoral College

The Electoral College is a process that was designed by the writers of the Constitution to elect presidents. It came from a compromise between the President being elected directly by the people and the President being chosen by Congress. Combining these ideas, the American people vote for a "college" of electors, who then meet to choose the President. Today, the people of each of the fifty states and the District of Columbia vote for the electors in November. The electors then officially vote for the President in December.

Q. What is the minimum voting age in the United States?

A. Eighteen

For most of U.S. history, Americans had to be at least twenty-one years old to vote. By the 1970s, many people thought that if someone was old enough to fight in a war, he or she should be old enough to vote. So, in 1971 the Twenty-sixth Amendment changed the minimum voting age to eighteen.

Q. In what month do we vote for the President?

A. November

The Constitution did not set a standard national election day. There was no specified day until 1845. Congress set the Tuesday after the first Monday in November as Election Day. They chose Tuesday so that voters had a full day after Sunday to travel to the polls. At that time, for religious reasons, many Americans considered Sunday to be a strict day of rest. Travel on this day was not allowed.

Q. In what month is the new President inaugurated?

A. January

Before 1933, presidents were inaugurated on March 4th. This meant that there were four months between when new Presidents were elected and when they took office. This gave the new President enough time to make the long journey to Washington, DC. By the 1930s, with the invention of automobiles and speedy trains, it was much faster to travel. The Twentieth Amendment officially changed the date of inauguration to January 20th. Franklin Roosevelt was the first President inaugurated on this date.

Q. For how long is the President elected?

Four years

Early American leaders felt that the head of the British government, the king, had too much power. Because of this, they limited the powers of the head of the new U.S. government. They decided that the President would have to be elected by the people every four years.

Q. How many full terms can a President serve?

A. Two full terms

The first U.S. President, George Washington, only ran for President twice. Washington felt that one person should not serve as President for a very long time. Following this tradition, no future President served for more than two terms until Franklin D. Roosevelt. Roosevelt was elected to four terms. Not long after he died, the Constitution was amended so that a President could be elected two only terms.

Q. Who becomes President if the President dies while in office?

A. The Vice President

The Vice President is first in line to take over as President. This has happened eight times in U.S. history. William Henry Harrison died in office in 1841. Zachary Taylor died in office in 1850. Abraham Lincoln was killed in office in 1865. James Garfield was killed in office in 1881. William McKinley was killed in office in 1901. Warren Harding died in office in 1923. Franklin Roosevelt died in office in 1945. John F. Kennedy was killed in office in 1963.

Q. Who becomes President if both the President and Vice President die?

A. The Speaker of the House

The answer to this question has changed throughout history. At first, following a 1791 law, the Senate President Pro Tempore was second in line to become President after the Vice President. Later, Congress passed a law making the Secretary of State next in line if the President and Vice President died.

Q. What special group advises the President?

A. The Cabinet advises the President.

The Constitution says that the leaders of the executive departments should advise the President. These department leaders, most of them called Secretaries, make up the Cabinet. Throughout history, Presidents have been able to change who makes up the Cabinet. For instance, when Congress created the Department of Homeland Security, President George W. Bush added the leader of this department to his Cabinet.

Q. What is the name of the President's official home?

A. The White House

The White House was built between 1792 and 1800. George Washington helped choose its exact location and supervised its construction, but never actually lived there. America's second President, John Adams, was the first to live in the White House. Fourteen years after it was built, the White House was burned by British troops during the War of 1812. Another destructive fire took place there in 1929, when Herbert Hoover was President.

Q. Where is the White House located?

A. Washington, DC

When the Constitution established our nation in 1789, the District of Columbia did not exist. At that time, the capital was New York City. Congress soon began discussing the location of a permanent capital city. Within Congress, representatives of northern states fought bitterly against representatives of southern states. Each side wanted the capital to be in their region. Finally, with the Compromise of 1790, the north agreed to let the capital be in the south. In return, the north was relieved of some of the debt that they owed from the Revolutionary War.

Q. Who was the first President of the United States?

A. George Washington

We honor George Washington as the first President of the United States After leading the military campaign to win American independence, Washington played an important role in the nation's formation. He was elected leader of the convention that was held to create the Constitution. Later on, Washington's service as the first U.S. President set a tradition for future presidents to follow. Washington refused to hold office for more than two terms. This started the tradition of a President not serving more than two terms. This limit is now required by a Constitutional Amendment.

Q. Which President is called the "Father of our Country"?

A. George Washington

Washington was a brave military general, a respected leader of the American Revolution, and our first President. His leadership was very important during America's transition from war and revolution to stability under the new government. After his victory over the British army, Washington retired. He reluctantly left his retirement when problems arose with the new country's system of government. Washington helped lead the effort to create a Constitution for the United States.

Q. Which President was the first Commander-in-Chief of the U.S. Army and Navy?

A. George Washington

The writers of the Constitution argued over how much power the new President should have. They decided that the President's powers should be limited in many ways, but that the President should be Commander-in-Chief of the military. During the Revolutionary War, George Washington had been supreme commander of the military. From this position, he led the U.S. forces to victory. This helped make him a unanimous choice to be the first President and Commander-in-Chief.

Q. Who was President during the Civil War?

A. Abraham Lincoln

We honor Abraham Lincoln because he led the nation during the Civil War. The war began when a group of southern states, known as the Confederacy, tried to separate from the United States. They wanted to preserve slavery and their farm-based economic system. This system was threatened by the northern states. Lincoln was a lawyer, legislator, and celebrated speaker before he was President. He became nationally famous for his debates with Senator Stephen A. Douglas, which took place when Lincoln and Douglas ran against each other for Illinois' U.S. Senate seat in 1858. Lincoln was assassinated by John Wilkes Booth in 1865.

Q. What did the Emancipation Proclamation do?

A. The Emancipation Proclamation freed the slaves.

President Lincoln issued the Emancipation Proclamation in the middle of the Civil War, in 1863. It freed the slaves in the rebelling

Confederate states. In 1865, the northern soldiers, known as the Union soldiers, defeated the soldiers from the South, known as the Confederate soldiers. The bitter, bloody Civil War was over, and the Union was preserved. Soon afterwards, the Thirteenth Amendment made the abolition of slavery part of the Constitution.

Q. Who is the President of the United States today?
A. George W. Bush

George W. Bush is the forty-third President of the United States. He was the Governor of Texas before winning the presidential election of 2000. Bush won re-election for a second term four years later. His wife, called the "first lady," is Laura Bush.

Q. Who is the Vice President of the United States today?
A. Dick Cheney

Richard B. (Dick) Cheney is the forty-sixth Vice President of the United States. Vice President Cheney grew up in Wyoming. He later represented the people of Wyoming in the U.S. Congress. As Vice President, Cheney is President of the U.S. Senate and a top advisor to the President.

Q. What is the legislative branch of our Government?
A. Congress

The main job of Congress is to make federal laws. Congress is divided into two parts—the Senate and the House of Representatives. By dividing Congress into two parts, the Constitution put the checks and balances idea to work within the legislative branch. Each part of Congress makes sure that the other does not become too powerful. These two pieces of Congress "check" each other because both must agree for a law to be passed.

Q. What makes up Congress?

A. The Senate and the House of Representatives

Specific powers are assigned to each of these chambers. Only the Senate has the power to reject a treaty signed by the President and a person chosen to become a Supreme Court Justice. Only the House of Representatives has the power to begin considering a bill that makes Americans pay taxes. Also, only the House has the power to make a President go to trial for a crime against the United States. This is called impeachment.

Q. Who makes the Federal laws in the United States?

A. Congress

A federal law is a rule that all people living in the United States must follow. Every law begins as a proposal made by a member of Congress. Tax proposals must begin in the House. Other types of proposals can be made by any senator or representative. When the Senate or House writes a proposal, the proposal is called a bill. If the President signs the bill, it becomes a federal law.

Q. Who signs bills into law?

A. The President

A bill is a proposed law being considered by Congress. Both parts of Congress – the Senate and the House of Representatives – must pass the same version of the bill. When they do so, the bill goes to the President to be signed into law. The President does, however, have veto power. This means that the President can reject a bill passed by Congress. If two-thirds of the House and two-thirds of the Senate vote to pass the bill again, though, the bill becomes a law. This process is called overriding the President's veto.

Q. What is the United States Capitol?

A. The place where Congress meets

When Congress moved into the Capitol in 1800, much of the construction of the interior rooms was not complete. It took two more years before Congress set aside enough funding to finish construction. Soon after, when British troops invaded Washington during the War of 1812, they set fire to the Capitol. Luckily, a heavy rainstorm saved the building from being burned down. Rebuilding the Capitol was not completed until 1829.

Q. Who elects Congress?

A. The citizens of the United States

The nation is divided into 435 Congressional districts. The people of each district are represented by a member of the House of Representatives. The people of each state also vote for two U.S. Senators. The term of office for members of the House of Representatives is two years. The term for senators is six years. Before 1913, state legislatures elected the U.S. Senators to represent that state. Ever since then, however, the people of a state have directly elected their two senators.

Q. How many senators are there in Congress?

A. There are one hundred senators in Congress, two from each state.

One reason the Senate was created was to give states with fewer people equal power to states with many people. With two senators representing each state, states with small populations have the same Senate representation as states with large populations. In contrast, in the House, states with more people have more representatives and therefore more power.

Q. Why are there one hundred Senators in the United States Senate?

A. Each state elects two Senators.

The writers of the Constitution wanted the two parts of Congress to have different characters. By giving each state only two senators, the writers made sure that the Senate would be small. This would keep the Senate more orderly than the larger House of Representatives. As James Madison wrote in Federalist Paper #63, the Senate should be a "temperate and respectable body of citizens" that operates in a "cool and deliberate" way.

Q. How long is a term in Senate?

A. Six years.

The writers of the Constitution wanted senators to be independent from public opinion. A longer, six-year term would give them this protection. They also wanted the Senate to balance the two-year term of the members of the House, who would more closely be governed by public opinion. The Constitution puts no limit on the number of terms a senator may serve.

Q. How many times may a senator or congressman be re-elected?

A. There is no limit.

Several states, like California, have term limits for members of their state legislature. Also, several states have considered limiting the number of terms that their U.S. Senators and Representatives can serve. In 1995, the U.S. Supreme Court ruled that no state can do this. The Court stated that such a practice would weaken the national character of Congress. The only way that congressional terms could be limited is through an amendment to the U.S. Constitution.

Q. Name two senators from your state.

A. The answer to this question depends on where you live.

For a complete list of United States Senators and the states they represent, go to http://www.senate.gov.

Q. How many voting members are in the House of Representatives?

A. There are 435 voting members in the House of Representatives. The House has had 435 members since 1912. Since that year, however, the distribution among the states of those 435 members has changed. This is because the number of Representatives from each state is re-calculated every ten years. New information from the Census is used in this recalculation. If one state gains many residents while another state loses many, the first state could get one or more new Representatives, while the other state could lose one or more. But the overall number of U.S. Representatives does not change.

Q. For how long do we elect each member of the House of Representatives?

A. Two years

People living in a Representative's district are called constituents. Representatives tend to reflect the views of his or her constituents. If Representatives do not do this, they may be voted out of office. The writers of the Constitution believed that short two-year terms and frequent elections keep Representatives closer to their constituents and public opinion. The Constitution puts no limit on the number of terms a Representative may serve.

Q. What is the highest part of the judiciary branch of our Government?

A. The Supreme Court

Many different federal courts make up the judiciary branch. The Constitution created the Supreme Court, but gave Congress the right to create lower federal courts. District and appellate courts are two examples of lower courts. Decisions made by these courts can be reviewed and overturned by the higher-ranking Supreme Court. The lower courts are spread throughout the country in various districts and circuits.

Q. What is the highest court in the United States?

A. The Supreme Court

The U.S. Supreme Court exercises complete authority over all federal courts. It has the final word on cases heard in federal court. The Supreme Court's interpretations of federal laws and of the Constitution are final. The Supreme Court is limited, though, in its power over states. It cannot interpret state law or state constitutions. The Court can, however, decide that a state law conflicts with federal law or the U.S. Constitution and is, thus, invalid.

Q. What are the duties of the Supreme Court?

A. To interpret and explain the laws

The U.S. Supreme Court makes sure that laws are consistent with the Constitution. If they are not, the Court can declare them unconstitutional and therefore not valid. In this case, the laws are rejected. The Court has the last word on all cases that have to do with federal laws and treaties. It also rules on other cases, such as those between states.

Q. Who nominates judges for the Supreme Court?

A. The President

The process of nominating a Supreme Court Justice is an example of checks and balances. The executive branch has the power to choose the members of the judicial branch of the federal government. The legislative branch can check this power, since the Senate must confirm the President's nominee. However, once on the Court, the Justices have lifelong terms. Therefore, the judicial branch's power and independence is protected.

Q. How many Supreme Court Justices are there?

A. Nine.

The number of Justices is not established in the Constitution. In the past, there have been as many as ten Justices and as few as six Justices. Now, there are eight Associate Justices and one Chief Justice. The current Associate Justices are Ruth Bader Ginsburg,

David Souter, Clarence Thomas, Stephen Breyer, Antonin Scalia, John Paul Stevens, Anthony Kennedy, and Samuel Alito. The Chief Justice of the Supreme Court is John Roberts.

Q. Who is Chief Justice of the Supreme Court?

A. John G. Roberts, Jr.

John G. Roberts, Jr. is currently the seventeenth Chief Justice of the U.S. Supreme Court. President George W. Bush nominated him for this position following the death of former Chief Justice William Rehnquist in September 2005. At the age of fifty, Judge Roberts became the youngest Chief Justice since 1801, when John Marshall was confirmed at the age of 45. Previously, Judge Roberts served on the U.S. Court of Appeals for the District of Columbia Circuit.

Q. Can the Constitution be changed?

A. Yes

One of the great things about the U.S. Constitution is that it is flexible and can be changed. It is changed through the amendment process. This is why we often refer to it as the "living Constitution." The Constitution's writers wisely decided that amendments should be rare. Because of this, the amendment process is difficult and time-consuming. Still, the Constitution has been changed twenty-seven times, with the most recent amendment added in 1992.

Q. What do we call changes to the Constitution?

A. Amendments

It is not easy for the Constitution to be changed, or amended.

First, two-thirds of the Senate and two-thirds of the House of Representatives must vote to approve an amendment. Then, three-fourths of the states must also approve the amendment. This process is called ratification.

Q. What are the first ten amendments to the Constitution called?

A. The Bill of Rights

The first ten amendments to the Constitution, ratified in 1791, became known as the Bill of Rights. The Bill of Rights, using principles from the Declaration of Independence, guarantees the rights of individuals and limits government power. The first eight amendments set out individual rights, such as the freedom of expression, the right to bear arms, freedom from search without warrant, freedom to not be tried twice for the same crime, the right to not testify against yourself, the right to trial by a jury of peers, the right to an attorney, and protection against excessive fines and unusual punishments. The last two amendments in the Bill of Rights address the rights of the people in their relationship with the state and federal governments.

Q. What is the Bill of Rights?

A. The first ten amendments to the Constitution

When the Constitution was first written, it did not focus on individual rights. Its goal was to create the system and structure of government. Many Americans, including a group called the Anti-Federalists, wanted a specific list of things the government could not do. James Madison responded with a list of individual rights and limits of government. Some of these included citizens' rights to practice their religion freely, to speak and publish freely, and to complain publicly about anything they wanted. The list was in the form of changes, or amendments, to the Constitution. These amendments were ratified in 1791. They soon became known as the Bill of Rights.

Q. Whose rights are guaranteed by the Constitution and the Bill of Rights?

A. All people living in the United States

One reason that millions of immigrants have come to America is this guarantee of rights. The Fifth Amendment guarantees everyone in the United States equal protection under the law. This is true no matter what color your skin is, what language you speak, or what religion you practice. The Fourteenth Amendment, ratified after the Civil War, expanded this guarantee of rights. No state would be able to block the rights of any of its citizens.

Q. Where does freedom of speech come from?

A. The Bill of Rights

Freedom of speech is a very important civil liberty. The very first section of the Bill of Rights, the First Amendment, guarantees this freedom. Speech includes speaking, writing, performing, and other ways of expressing yourself. Americans have the basic right to express their views on any subject. This is true even if the government disagrees with these views. However, in certain very specific situations, freedom of expression is limited. For example, no one can falsely shout "fire" in a theater to cause panic.

Q. Name one right or freedom guaranteed by the First Amendment.

A. The rights of freedom of religion, of speech, of the press, of assembly, and to petition the government.

These First Amendment rights are all part of a person's freedom of expression. Protecting free expression promotes open dialogue and debate on public issues, which is the foundation of democracy. Similarly, the free flow of ideas facilitates peaceful change and advances knowledge. Also in the First Amendment, freedom of religion has two parts. It blocks Congress from setting up an official U.S. religion, and it protects citizens' rights to hold any religious belief or none at all.

Q. How many changes, or amendments, are there to the Constitution?

A. Twenty-seven

The first amendments to the Constitution were added in 1791. These original ten Amendments are called the Bill of Rights. Since the Bill of Rights was created, seventeen more amendments have been added. The twenty-seventh amendment is the most recent addition. It was added in 1992, and addresses how senators and representatives are paid.

Q. Name the amendments that guarantee or address voting rights.

The 15th, 19th, 24th and 26th amendments

The Nineteenth Amendment gave women the ability to vote. It was a result of decades of hard work by the women's rights movement. This was also known as the women's suffrage movement.

The Fifteenth Amendment was written after the Civil War and the end of slavery. It allowed all American men of all races to vote. Some leaders of southern states were upset that the Fifteenth Amendment allowed African-Americans to vote. These leaders designed fees called poll taxes to stop them from voting. The Twenty-fourth Amendment made it illegal to stop someone from voting because he or she did not pay a poll tax. The Twenty-sixth Amendment lowered the voting age to eighteen.

Q. What is the most important right granted to United States citizens?

A. The right to vote

No American is required by law to vote, but exercising your right to vote is a very important part of citizenship. Only by voting can your voice be heard. By voting, you actively commit yourself to the democratic process. Citizens vote to be represented by leaders who share their ideas and stand up for their interests. Constitutional amendments such as the Fifteenth Amendment (giving former slaves the right to vote) and the Nineteenth Amendment (giving women the right to vote) greatly improved our democracy by allowing more groups of citizens to vote.

Q. Name one benefit of being a citizen of the United States.

A. To obtain federal government jobs, to travel with a U.S. passport, or to petition for close relatives to come to the United States to live.

Former Chief Justice of the Supreme Court Earl Warren once said that citizenship is "nothing less than the right to have rights."

Some of the most important of these are the right to choose your job, speak freely about your beliefs, and disagree with government policies. At the same time, citizen responsibilities include obeying the law, voting, and serving on juries. Responsible citizens also take part in their communities. This might mean joining the Parent Teacher Association (PTA) of your child's school, running for a position on the local school board, or volunteering to help at a polling station.

Q. How many states are there in the United States today?

A. Fifty states.

There are fifty states in the U.S. The first thirteen states, which were the original thirteen colonies, were Connecticut, New Hampshire, New York, New Jersey, Maryland, Virginia, Pennsylvania, Rhode Island, Massachusetts, Georgia, Delaware, North Carolina, and South Carolina. The last state to join the Union was Hawaii.

Q. What was the forty-ninth state added to the United States?

A. Alaska

In 1867, the U.S. government bought the land of Alaska from Russia, paying $7,200,000. Secretary of State William Seward made the decision to buy Alaska. Ninety-two years later, in 1959, Alaska finally became a state. The people of Alaska now honor Seward for his commitment to their state. They celebrate Seward's Day every March.

Q. What was the fiftieth state to be added to the United States?

A. Hawaii

Hawaii is the only state completely separated from the continent of North America. There are six major islands and many smaller ones in this state. Hawaii is located in the Pacific Ocean, about 2,400 miles from Los Angeles, California. The islands officially became a U.S. territory in 1898. For many decades after this, Hawaiians pushed for Congress to make the territory a state, which finally happened in 1959.

Q. What is the capital of the state you live in?

A. The answer to this question depends on the state where you reside.

To learn the capital of your state, go to **www.firstgov.gov** and select the state government link.

Q. What is the executive of a state government called?

A. The Governor

The position of governor is not the same in every state. The number of years that a governor is elected to serve—called a term—may differ from state to state. The governor's job within a state government is similar to the President's job within the federal government. However, the state laws that a governor carries out are different from the federal laws that the President carries out. The Constitution says that certain issues are covered by federal, not state, laws. All other issues are covered by state laws. This system is known as federalism. Federalism forces states and the federal government to share power on many issues.

Q. Who is the current governor of the state you live in?

A. The answer to this question depends on where you live.

To learn the name of the Governor of your state, go to **www.firstgov.gov** and select the state government link.

Q. What is the head executive of a city government called?

A. The Mayor

Like a governor or the President, a mayor usually shares power with a legislative body. In city government, this is often called the City Council. Cities in the United States are located within larger regions called counties. Usually, each county has its own government.

Q. What group has the power to declare war?

A. Congress

Congress has formally declared war eleven times. The Senate vote for war was very close two of these times. These close votes took place before the War of 1812 and the Spanish-American War. Congress has not declared war since the United States entered World War II in 1941. However, seven times since then Congress has authorized military action. This step reflects the democratic tradition of the legislative branch approving the President's use of troops.

Q. Who is Commander-in-Chief of the United States military?

A. The President

Making the President the Commander-in-Chief shows the founding fathers' commitment to democratic ideals.

Q. Name some countries that were our enemies during World War II.

A. Germany, Italy, and Japan

The United States officially went to war on December 8, 1941. President Franklin D. Roosevelt, as commander-in-chief of the military, obtained an official declaration of war from Congress. This was the day after Japan bombed Pearl Harbor, an American naval base in Hawaii. Japan's partners in the Axis, Italy and Germany, then declared war on the United States, Great Britain, and their allies. The Allies fought against the German Nazis, the Italian Fascists, and Japan's military empire. This was very difficult for the United States, which had to fight wars in both the Pacific region and Europe.

Q. Name one of the purposes of the United Nations.

A. For countries to discuss and try to resolve world problems or to provide economic aid to many countries

The United Nations, often called the U.N., was established in 1945, soon after World War II ended. The Charter of the United Nations names the main functions of the U.N.—"to maintain international peace and security...to develop friendly relations among nations...(and) to achieve international cooperation in solving international problems." The two best-known parts of the U.N. are the General Assembly, made up of over 190 countries, and the Security Council, with only ten countries. The United States is one of five countries that is a permanent member of the Security Council. The President has the power to choose the Ambassador of the United States to the United Nations. The Senate must then confirm this choice.

Q. Who was Martin Luther King, Jr.?

A. A civil rights leader

Martin Luther King, Jr. was a Baptist minister and civil rights hero. During his short life, he worked hard to make America a more fair, tolerant, and equal nation. King believed in the ideals of the Declaration of Independence. He advanced the idea that every citizen deserves America's promise of equality and justice.

APPENDIX E: SAMPLE RECEIPT NOTICE

Department of Homeland Security
U.S. Citizenship and Immigration Services

I-797C, Notice of Action

THE UNITED STATES OF AMERICA

Receipt			NOTICE DATE September 14, 2006
CASE TYPE N400 Application For Naturalization			USCIS A# A
APPLICATION NUMBER LIN*	RECEIVED DATE September 07, 2006	PRIORITY DATE September 07, 2006	PAGE 1 of 1

APPLICANT NAME AND MAILING ADDRESS	PAYMENT INFORMATION:
c/o DEBBIE M SCHELL 780 LEE STREET SUITE 102 DES PLAINES IL 60016	Single Application Fee: $400.00 Total Amount Received: $400.00 Total Balance Due: $0.00

The above application has been received by our office and is in process. Our records indicate your personal information is as follows:

Date of Birth: December 21, 1969
Address Where You Live:

Please verify your personal information listed above and immediately notify our office at the address or phone number listed below if there are any changes.

You will be notified of the date and place of your interview when you have been scheduled by the local USCIS office. You should expect to be notified within 540 days of this notice.

If you have any questions or comments regarding this notice or the status of your case, please contact our office at the below address or customer service number. You will be notified separately about any other cases you may have filed.

If you have other questions about possible immigration benefits and services, filing information, or USCIS forms, please call the USCIS National Customer Service Center (NCSC) at **1-800-375-5283**. If you are hearing impaired, please call the NCSC TDD at **1-800-767-1833**.

If you have access to the Internet, you can also visit USCIS at **www.uscis.gov**. Here you can find valuable information about forms and filing instructions, and about general immigration services and benefits. At present, this site does not provide case status information.

USCIS Office Address:
U.S. CITIZENSHIP AND IMMIGRATION SERVICES
PO BOX 87400
LINCOLN NE 68501-

USCIS Customer Service Number:
(800) 375-5283

REPRESENTATIVE COPY

LIN$

● *Please save this notice for your records. Please enclose a copy if you have to write us or a U. S. Consulate about this case, or if you file another application based on this decision.*

● *You will be notified separately about any other applications or petitions you have filed.*

Additional Information

GENERAL.

The filing of an application or petition does not in itself allow a person to enter the United States and does not confer any other right or benefit.

INQUIRIES.

You should contact the office listed on the reverse side of this notice if you have questions about the notice, or questions about the status of your application or petition. *We recommend you call.* However, if you write us, please enclose a copy of this notice with your letter.

APPROVAL OF NONIMMIGRANT PETITION.

Approval of a nonimmigrant petition means that the person for whom it was filed has been found eligible for the requested classification. If this notice indicated we are notifying a U.S. Consulate about the approval for the purpose of visa issuance, and you or the person you filed for have questions about visa issuance, please contact the appropriate U.S. Consulate directly.

APPROVAL OF AN IMMIGRANT PETITION.

Approval of an immigrant petition does not convey any right or status. The approved petition simply establishes a basis upon which the person you filed for can apply for an immigrant or fiance(e) visa or for adjustment of status.

A person is not guaranteed issuance of a visa or a grant of adjustment simply because this petition is approved. Those processes look at additional criteria.

If this notice indicates we have approved the immigrant petition you filed, and have forwarded it to the Department of State Immigrant Visa Processing Center, that office will contact the person you filed the petition for directly with information about visa issuance.

In addition to the information on the reverse of this notice, the instructions for the petition you filed provide additional information about processing after approval of the petition.

For more information about whether a person who is already in the U.S. can apply for adjustment of status, please see Form I-485, *Application to Register Permanent Residence or Adjust Status.*

APPENDIX F:
SAMPLE NOTICE TO APPEAR FOR FINGERPRINTING

Department of Homeland Security
U.S. Citizenship and Immigration Services

I-797C, Notice of Action

THE UNITED STATES OF AMERICA

Fingerprint Notification			NOTICE DATE September 18, 2006
CASE TYPE N400 Application For Naturalization			USCIS A# A
APPLICATION NUMBER LIN*	RECEIVED DATE September 07, 2006	PRIORITY DATE September 07, 2006	PAGE 1 of 1

APPLICANT NAME AND MAILING ADDRESS

c/o DEBBIE M SCHELL
780 LEE STREET SUITE 102
DES PLAINES IL 60016

lldllldlllllllllll

To process your application, USCIS must take your fingerprints and have them cleared by the FBI. **PLEASE APPEAR AT THE BELOW APPLICATION SUPPORT CENTER AT THE DATE AND TIME SPECIFIED.** If you are unable to do so, complete the bottom of this notice and return the entire original notice to the address below. **RESCHEDULING YOUR APPOINTMENT WILL DELAY YOUR APPLICATION. IF YOU FAIL TO APPEAR AS SCHEDULED BELOW OR FAIL TO REQUEST RESCHEDULING, YOUR APPLICATION WILL BE CONSIDERED ABANDONED.**

APPLICATION SUPPORT CENTER CIS NAPERVILLE 888 SOUTH ROUTE 59 #124 NAPERVILLE IL 60540	DATE AND TIME OF APPOINTMENT 09/27/2006 09:00 AM

WHEN YOU GO TO THE APPLICATION SUPPORT CENTER TO HAVE YOUR FINGERPRINTS TAKEN, YOU MUST BRING:
1. THIS APPOINTMENT NOTICE and
2. PHOTO IDENTIFICATION. Naturalization applicants must bring their Alien Registration Card. All other applicants must bring a passport, driver's license, national ID, military ID, or State-issued photo ID. If you appear without proper identification, you will not be fingerprinted.

PLEASE DISREGARD THIS NOTICE IF YOUR APPLICATION HAS ALREADY BEEN GRANTED.

REQUEST FOR RESCHEDULING

Please reschedule my appointment for the next available: ☐ Wednesday afternoon   ☐ Saturday afternoon

USCIS cannot guarantee the day preferred, but will do so to the extent possible.
Upon receipt of your request, you will be provided a new appointment notice. Please mail your request to:

CIS NAPERVILLE
888 SOUTH ROUTE 59
#124
NAPERVILLE IL 60540

If you have any questions regarding this notice, please call 1-800-375-5283.   REPRESENTATIVE COPY

APPLICATION NUMBER
LIN*

WARNING!
Due to limited seating availability in our lobby areas, only persons who are necessary to assist with transportation or completing the fingerprint worksheet should accompany you.

● *Please save this notice for your records. Please enclose a copy if you have to write us or a U. S. Consulate about this case, or if you file another application based on this decision.*

● *You will be notified separately about any other applications or petitions you have filed.*

Additional Information

GENERAL.

The filing of an application or petition does not in itself allow a person to enter the United States and does not confer any other right or benefit.

INQUIRIES.

You should contact the office listed on the reverse side of this notice if you have questions about the notice, or questions about the status of your application or petition. *We recommend you call.* However, if you write us, please enclose a copy of this notice with your letter.

APPROVAL OF NONIMMIGRANT PETITION.

Approval of a nonimmigrant petition means that the person for whom it was filed has been found eligible for the requested classification. If this notice indicated we are notifying a U.S. Consulate about the approval for the purpose of visa issuance, and you or the person you filed for have questions about visa issuance, please contact the appropriate U.S. Consulate directly.

APPROVAL OF AN IMMIGRANT PETITION.

Approval of an immigrant petition does not convey any right or status. The approved petition simply establishes a basis upon which the person you filed for can apply for an immigrant or fiance(e) visa or for adjustment of status.

A person is not guaranteed issuance of a visa or a grant of adjustment simply because this petition is approved. Those processes look at additional criteria.

If this notice indicates we have approved the immigrant petition you filed, and have forwarded it to the Department of State Immigrant Visa Processing Center, that office will contact the person you filed the petition for directly with information about visa issuance.

In addition to the information on the reverse of this notice, the instructions for the petition you filed provide additional information about processing after approval of the petition.

For more information about whether a person who is already in the U.S. can apply for adjustment of status, please see Form I-485, *Application to Register Permanent Residence or Adjust Status*.

APPENDIX G:
SAMPLE NOTICE TO APPEAR FOR NATURALIZATION INITIAL INTERVIEW

Department of Homeland Security
U.S. Citizenship and Immigration Services

I-797C, Notice of Action

THE UNITED STATES OF AMERICA

Request for Applicant to Appear for Naturalization Initial Interview	NOTICE DATE October 13, 2006

CASE TYPE		USCIS A#
N400 Application For Naturalization		A

APPLICATION NUMBER	RECEIVED DATE	PRIORITY DATE	PAGE
LIN*	September 07, 2006	September 07, 2006	1 of 1

APPLICANT NAME AND MAILING ADDRESS

c/o DEBBIE M SCHELL
780 LEE STREET SUITE 102
DES PLAINES IL 60016

.ll..ll...ll....ll.ll..

Please come to:
U.S. CITIZENSHIP & IMMIGRATION SERVICES
101 WEST CONGRESS PARKWAY
CITIZENSHIP OFFICE
3RD FLOOR
CHICAGO IL 60605
On (Date):   Tuesday, November 28, 2006
At (Time):   01:40 PM

You are hereby notified to appear for an interview on your Application for Naturalization at the date, time, and place indicated above. **Waiting room capacity is limited. Please do not arrive any earlier than 30 minutes before your scheduled appointment time.** The proceeding will take about two hours. If for any reason you cannot keep this appointment, return this letter immediately to the USCIS office address listed below with your explanation and a request for a new appointment; otherwise, no further action will be taken on your application.

If you are applying for citizenship for yourself, you will be tested on your knowledge of the government and history of the United States. You will also be tested on reading, writing, and speaking English, unless on the day you filed your application, you have been living in the United States for a total of at least 20 years as a lawful permanent resident and are over 50 years old, or you have been living in the United States for a total of 15 years as a lawful permanent resident and are over 55 years old, or unless you have a medically determinable disability (you must have filed form N648 Medical Certification for Disability Exception, with your N400 Application for Naturalization).

You MUST BRING the following with you to the interview:
- This letter.
- Your Alien Registration Card (green card).
- Any evidence of Selective Service Registration.
- Your passport and/or any other documents you used in connection with any entries into the United States.
- Those items noted below which are applicable to you:

If applying for NATURALIZATION AS THE SPOUSE of a United States Citizen;
- Your marriage certificate.
- Proof of death or divorce for each prior marriage of yourself or spouse.
- Your spouse's birth or naturalization certificate or certificate of citizenship.

If applying for NATURALIZATION as a member of the United States Armed Forces;
- Your discharge certificate, or form DD 214.

If copies of a document were submitted as evidence with your N400 application, the originals of those documents should be brought to the interview.

PLEASE keep this appointment, even if you do not have all the items indicated above.

If you have any questions or comments regarding this notice or the status of your case, please contact our office at the below address or customer service number. You will be notified separately about any other cases you may have filed.

USCIS Office Address:
U.S. CITIZENSHIP AND IMMIGRATION SERVICES
USCIS CHICAGO DISTRICT OFFICE
101 WEST CONGRESS PARKWAY
CHICAGO IL 60605-

USCIS Customer Service Number:
(800) 375-5283

REPRESENTATIVE COPY

- *Please save this notice for your records. Please enclose a copy if you have to write us or a U. S. Consulate about this case, or if you file another application based on this decision.*

- *You will be notified separately about any other applications or petitions you have filed.*

Additional Information

GENERAL.

The filing of an application or petition does not in itself allow a person to enter the United States and does not confer any other right or benefit.

INQUIRIES.

You should contact the office listed on the reverse side of this notice if you have questions about the notice, or questions about the status of your application or petition. *We recommend you call.* However, if you write us, please enclose a copy of this notice with your letter.

APPROVAL OF NONIMMIGRANT PETITION.

Approval of a nonimmigrant petition means that the person for whom it was filed has been found eligible for the requested classification. If this notice indicated we are notifying a U.S. Consulate about the approval for the purpose of visa issuance, and you or the person you filed for have questions about visa issuance, please contact the appropriate U.S. Consulate directly.

APPROVAL OF AN IMMIGRANT PETITION.

Approval of an immigrant petition does not convey any right or status. The approved petition simply establishes a basis upon which the person you filed for can apply for an immigrant or fiance(e) visa or for adjustment of status.

A person is not guaranteed issuance of a visa or a grant of adjustment simply because this petition is approved. Those processes look at additional criteria.

If this notice indicates we have approved the immigrant petition you filed, and have forwarded it to the Department of State Immigrant Visa Processing Center, that office will contact the person you filed the petition for directly with information about visa issuance.

In addition to the information on the reverse of this notice, the instructions for the petition you filed provide additional information about processing after approval of the petition.

For more information about whether a person who is already in the U.S. can apply for adjustment of status, please see Form I-485, *Application to Register Permanent Residence or Adjust Status.*

Department of Homeland Security
U.S. Citizenship and Immigration Services

N-659, Naturalization Interview
Document Check List

NOTICE TO NATURALIZATION APPLICANTS.

Please bring the **original and a photocopy** of the applicable items listed below to your naturalization interview. Any document in a foreign language must be accompanied by an English language translation. The translator must certify that he or she is competent to translate and that the translation is accurate.

You should be on time for your interview because rescheduling will cause delays in processing your case.

DOCUMENT CHECK LIST.

1. All applicants must bring:

- Your Permanent Resident Card (previously known as "Alien Registration Card" or "Green Card"); **and**
- Photo identification; **and**
- Your passport and any travel documents issued by the U.S. Government.

2. If your current name is different than the name on your Permanent Resident Card, bring:

- The document that legally changed your name (e.g., marriage license, divorce decree, court document).

3. If you are applying for naturalization on the basis of marriage to a U.S. citizen, bring:

- Proof that your spouse has been a U.S. citizen for at least the past three years (birth certificate, naturalization certificate, certificate of citizenship, your spouse's valid U.S. passport, **or** Form FS240, "Report of Birth Abroad of a Citizen of the United States of America"); **and**
- Your current marriage certificate; **and**
- Proof of termination of **all** of your spouse's prior marriages (e.g., divorce decree, death certificate); **and**
- An **original** Internal Revenue Service (IRS) Form 1722 listing tax information for the past three years (call IRS toll-free at **1-800-829-1040**), **or** copies of the income tax forms you filed for the past three years.

4. If you were previously married, bring:

- Proof of termination of **all** of your prior marriages (e.g., divorce decree, death certificate).

5. If you have ever been in the U.S. military, are applying based on military service (see the Immigration and Nationality Act, sections 328 and 329), and have not previously submitted the two forms listed below with your Form N-400, bring:

- An **original** Form N-426, "Request for Certification of Military or Naval Service;" **and**
- An **original** Form G-325B, "Biographic Information."

6. If you have taken a trip outside of the United States that lasted for six months or more since becoming a Permanent Resident, bring:

- An **original** IRS 1722 letter (call IRS toll-free at **1-800-829-1040**), listing tax information for the past five years (or for the past three years if you are applying on the basis of marriage to a U.S. citizen).

7. If you have a dependent spouse or children and have been ordered to provide financial support, bring:

- Copies of the court or government order to provide financial support; **and**
- Evidence that you have complied with the court or government order (cancelled checks, money order receipts, a court or agency printout of child support payments **or** evidence of wage garnishments).

(Continued on Next Page)

8. **If you have ever been arrested or detained by any law enforcement officer for any reason and <u>no</u> charges were filed, bring:**

   - An official statement from the arresting agency or applicable court indicating that no charges were filed.

9. **If you have ever been arrested or detained by any law enforcement officer for any reason and <u>charges</u> were filed, bring:**

   - An **original** or certified copy of the arrest record(s) and the complete court disposition for each incident (dismissal order, conviction record **or** acquittal order).

10. **If you have ever been convicted or placed in an alternative sentencing program or rehabilitative program bring:**

    - The sentencing record for each incident; **and**

    - Evidence that you completed your sentence (probation record, parole record **or** evidence that you completed an alternative sentencing program or rehabilitative program).

11. **If you have ever had any arrest or conviction vacated, set aside, sealed, expunged or otherwise removed from your record, bring:**

    - An **original** or a certified copy of the court order, vacating, setting aside, sealing, expunging or otherwise removing the arrest or conviction.

    Note that unless a traffic incident was alcohol or drug related, you do not need to submit documentation for traffic fines and incidents that did not involve an actual arrest if the only penalty was a fine of less than $500 and/or points on your driver's license.

12. **If you have any federal, state or local taxes that are overdue, bring:**

    - A signed agreement from the IRS, state or local tax office showing that you have filed a tax return and arranged to pay the taxes you owe; **and**

    Documentation from the IRS, state or local tax office showing the current status of your repayment program.

13. **If you are applying for a disability exception to the testing requirement and have not submitted Form N-648, bring:**

    - An **original** Form N-648, "Medical Certification for Disability Exceptions," completed by a licensed medical doctor, licensed clinical psychologist or licensed doctor of osteopathy.

14. **If you did not register with the Selective Service and you (1) are male, (2) over 26 years old, (3) were born on or after January 1, 1960 and (4) were a Permanent Resident between the ages of 18 and 26 when you failed to register, bring:**

    - A "Status Information Letter" from the Selective Service. (Call **1-888-688-6888** for more information).

NOTE: Please bring the required documents to avoid delays in processing your case. This is a general check list. Since each case is unique, you may be required to submit additional documentation.

APPENDIX H:
REQUEST FOR A HEARING ON A DECISION IN NATURALIZATION PROCEEDINGS

OMB No. 1615-0050; Expires 7/31/07

N-336, Request for a Hearing on a Decision in Naturalization Proceedings
(Under Section 336 of the INA)

Department of Homeland Security
U.S. Citizenship and Immigration Services

Instructions

1. Filing This Form.

This form is used to appeal an unfavorable decision for an individual applicant.

You must file your request for a hearing within 30 calendar days after service of the decision (33 days if your decision was mailed) with the local office of the U.S. Citizenship and Immigration Services (USCIS) that made the unfavorable decision.

The date of service is normally the date of the decision. Submit an original request only. Additional copies are not required. (USCIS is comprised of offices of former Immigration and Naturalization Service.)

2. What Is the Fee?

You must pay a fee of **$265.00** to file this form.

The fee will not be refunded, regardless of the action taken in your case. Do not mail cash. All checks or money orders, whether United States or foreign, must be payable in U.S. currency at a financial institution in the United States. When a check is drawn on the account of a person other than yourself, write your name on the face of the check. If the check is not honored, USCIS will charge you $30.00.

Pay by check or money order in the exact amount. Make the check or money order payable to the **Department of Homeland Security**; unless:

- If you live in Guam and are filing this form there, make the check or money order payable to the "Treasurer, Guam."

- If you live in the U.S. Virgin Islands and are filing this form there, make the check or money order payable to the "Commissioner of Finance of the Virgin Islands."

When preparing your check or money order, spell out Department of Homeland Security. Do not use the initials "USDHS" or "DHS."

How to Check If the Fee Is Correct.

The fee on this form is current as of the edition date appearing in the lower right corner of this page. However, because USCIS fees change periodically, you can verify if the fee is correct by following one of the steps below:

- Visit our website at **www.uscis.gov** and scroll down to "Forms and E-Filing" to check the appropriate fee, or

- Review the Fee Schedule included in your form package, if you called us to request the form, or

- Telephone our National Customer Service Center at **1-800-375-5283** and ask for the fee information.

3. Attorney or Representative.

If you wish, you may be represented, at no expense to the U.S. government, by an attorney or other duly authorized representative. If so, that person must submit a Notice of Appearance (Form G-28) with the request for a hearing. Form G-28 can be obtained by calling our forms line number at **1-800-870-3676**, our National Customer Service Center at **1-800-375-5283** or from our internet website at **www.uscis.gov**.

4. Brief.

You do not need to submit a brief in support of your request, but you may submit two briefs if you so choose. You may also submit a simple written statement instead of a brief. You may also submit evidence. You must send your request and accompanying fee and documentation to the USCIS office that made the unfavorable decision. If you need more than 30 days, you must, within the initial 30 day period, explain why in a separate letter attached to this form. USCIS may grant more time for good cause.

5. Use InfoPass for Appointments.

As an alternative to waiting in line for assistance at your local USCIS office, you can now schedule an appointment through our internet-based system, **InfoPass**. To access the system, visit our website at **www.uscis.gov**. Use the **InfoPass** appointment scheduler and follow the screen prompts to set up your appointment. **InfoPass** generates an electronic appointment notice that appears on the screen. Print the notice and take it with you to your appointment. The notice gives the time and date of your appointment, along with the address of the USCIS office.

6. Paperwork Reduction Act Notice.

A person is not required to respond to a collection of information unless it displays a currently valid OMB control number. This collection of information is estimated to average 2 hours and 45 minutes per response, including the time for reviewing instructions, gathering evidence, completing the form, and appearing for an interview. Send comments regarding this burden estimate or any other aspect of this collection of information, including suggestions for reducing this burden, to: U.S. Citizenship and Immigration Services, Regulatory Management Division, 111 Massachusetts Avenue, N.W., Washington, DC 20529; OMB No.1615-0050. **Do not mail your completed application to this address.**

OMB No. 1615-0050; Expires 7/31/07

N-336, Request for a Hearing on a Decision in Naturalization Proceedings (Under Section 336 of the INA)

Department of Homeland Security
U.S. Citizenship and Immigration Services

For USCIS Only	
Decision: ☐ Grant ☐ Denial	Fee:
1. In the Matter of: (Name of Naturalization Applicant)	File Number: **A-**

2. I am filing a request for hearing on the decision dated:

3. Please check the one block that applies:

a. ☐ I am **not submitting** a separate brief, statement or evidence.

b. ☐ I am **submitting** a separate brief, statement and/or evidence with this form.

c. ☐ I need _____ days to submit a brief, statement and/or evidence to the USCIS. (May be granted only for good cause shown. Explain in a separate letter.)

4. Person filing request:

Name (Type or print in black ink.)

Address (Street Number and Name)   (Apt. Number)

(City)   (State)   (Zip Code)

Signature   Date (mm/dd/yyyy)

☐ I am an attorney or representative and I represent the applicant requesting a hearing on a naturalization proceeding. [You must attach a Notice or Entry or Appearance (Form G-28) if you are an attorney or representative and did not previously submit such a form.]

(Person for whom you are appearing)

5. Briefly state the reason(s) for this request for a hearing:

_____

_____

_____

_____

_____

_____

APPENDIX I:
COUNTRIES THAT ALLOW SOME TYPE OF DUAL CITIZENSHIP

1. Albania
2. Angola
3. Antigua and Barbuda
4. Argentina
5. Australia
6. Bahamas
7. Bangladesh
8. Barbados
9. Belarus
10. Belize
11. Bolivia
12. Benin
13. Braziz
14. Bulgaria
15. Burkina Faso
16. Cambodia
17. Canada
18. Cape Verde
19. Chile
20. Columbia
21. Costa Rica
22. Croatia
23. Cyprus
24. Cyprus (North)
25. Czech Republic
26. Dominica
27. Dominican Republic
28. Ecuador
29. Egypt
30. El Salvador
31. Estonia
32. Federal Republic of Yugoslavia
33. Fiji
34. France

35. Germany
36. Ghana
37. Greece
38. Grenada
39. Guatemala
40. Guyana
41. Haiti
42. Hungary
43. India
44. Iran
45. Ireland
46. Israel
47. Italy
48. Jamaica
49. Jordan
50. Latvia
51. Lebanon
52. Lesotho
53. Liechtenstein
54. Lithuania
55. Macao
56. Macedonia
57. Madagascar
58. Malta
59. Mexico
60. Montenegro
61. Mongolia
62. Morocco
63. Netherlands
64. New Zealand
65. Nicaragua
66. Nigeria
67. Northern Ireland
68. Panama

69. Pakistan
70. Paraguay
71. Peru
72. Pitcairn
73. Philippines
74. Poland
75. Portugal
76. Romania
77. Russia
78. Saint Kitts, (Saint Christopher) and Nevis
79. Saint Lucia
80. Saint Vincent
81. Serbia
82. Slovenia
83. South Africa
84. Spain
85. Sri Lanka
86. Sweden
87. Switzerland
88. Syria
89. Taiwan
90. Thailand
91. Tonga
92. Tibet
93. Trinidad and Tobago
94. Turkey
95. United Kingdom
96. Ukraine
97. Uruguay
98. Vietnam
99. Western Samoa
100. Yemen

APPENDIX J: GLOSSARY OF TERMS

acquired citizenship. Citizenship conferred at birth on children born abroad to a U.S. citizen parent(s).

acquired citizenship. Citizenship conferred at birth on children born abroad to a U.S. citizen parent(s).

adjustment to immigrant status. Procedure allowing certain aliens already in the United States to apply for immigrant status. Aliens admitted to the United States in a nonimmigrant, refugee, or parolee category may have their status changed to that of lawful permanent resident if they are eligible to receive an immigrant visa and one is immediately available. In such cases, the alien is counted as an immigrant as of the date of adjustment, even though the alien may have been in the United States for an extended period of time. Beginning in October 1994, section 245(i) of the INA allowed illegal residents who were eligible for immigrant status to remain in the United States and adjust to permanent resident status by applying at a USCIS office and paying an additional penalty fee. Section 245(i) is no longer available unless the alien is the beneficiary of a petition under section 204 of the Act or of an application for a labor certification under section 212(a)(5)(A), filed on or before April 30, 2001. And, if filed after January 1, 1998, the alien must have been present in the United States on December 21, 2000. Prior to October 1994, most illegal residents were required to leave the United States and acquire a visa abroad from the Department of State as they are again now.

alien. Any person not a citizen or national of the United States.

certificate of citizenship. Identity document proving U.S. citizenship. Certificates of citizenship are issued to derivative citizens and to persons who acquired U.S. citizenship.

conditional resident. Any alien granted permanent resident status on a conditional basis (e.g., a spouse of a U.S. citizen; an immigrant investor), who is required to petition for the removal of the set conditions before the second anniversary of the approval of his or her conditional status.

crime of moral turpitude. A crime that involves doing something wrong that the person committing the crime should have known was wrong.

derivative citizenship. Citizenship conveyed to children through the naturalization of parents or, under certain circumstances, to foreign-born children adopted by U.S. citizen parents, provided certain conditions are met.

general naturalization provisions. The basic requirements for naturalization that every applicant must meet, unless a member of a special class. General provisions require an applicant to be at least 18 years of age and a lawful permanent resident with five years of continuous residence in the United States, have been physically present in the country for half that period, and establish good moral character for at least that period.

lawful permanent resident (LPR). Any person not a citizen of the United States who is residing the in the U.S. under legally recognized and lawfully recorded permanent residence as an immigrant. Also known as "Permanent Resident Alien," "Resident Alien Permit Holder," and "Green Card Holder."

naturalization. The conferring, by any means, of citizenship upon a person after birth

naturalization application. The form used by a lawful permanent resident to apply for U.S. citizenship. The application is filed with U.S. Citizenship and Immigration Services at the Service Center with jurisdiction over the applicant's place of residence.

permanent resident alien. An alien admitted to the United States as a lawful permanent resident. Permanent residents are also commonly referred to as immigrants; however, the Immigration and Nationality Act (INA) broadly defines an immigrant as any alien in the United States, except one legally admitted under specific nonimmigrant categories (INA section 101(a)(15)). An illegal alien who entered the United States without inspection, for example, would be strictly defined as an immigrant under the INA but is not a permanent resident alien. Lawful permanent residents are legally accorded the privilege of residing permanently in the United States. They may be issued immigrant visas by the Department of State overseas or adjusted to permanent resident status by U.S. Citizenship and Immigration Services in the United States.

resident alien. Applies to non-U.S. citizens currently residing in the United States. The term is applied in three different manners; please see *permanent resident, conditional resident,* and *returning resident.*

returning resident. Any Lawful Permanent Resident who has been outside the United States and is returning to the U.S. Also defined as a "special immigrant." If outside of the U.S. for more than 180 days, must apply for readmission to the U.S. If outside of the U.S. for more than one year and is returning to his or her permanent residence in the United States, usually must have a re-entry documentation from USCIS or an immigrant visa from the Department of State.

special immigrants. Certain categories of immigrants who were exempt from numerical limitation before fiscal year 1992 and subject to limitation under the employment-based fourth preference beginning in 1992; persons who lost citizenship by marriage; persons who lost citizenship by serving in foreign armed forces; ministers of religion and other religious workers, their spouses and children; certain employees and former employees of the U.S. Government abroad, their spouses and children; Panama Canal Act immigrants; certain foreign medical school graduates, their spouses and children; certain retired employees of international organizations, their spouses and children; juvenile court dependents; and certain aliens serving in the U.S. Armed Forces, their spouses and children.

INDEX

ABOUT THE AUTHORS

Kurt A. Wagner, MBA, JD (Magna Cum Laude) is an attorney, author, university lecturer, and founder of the Law Offices of Kurt A. Wagner with offices in Illinois and Austria. He is a member of the Immigration and International Law Section of the Illinois State Bar Association, the Chicago Bar Association, and the Washington, D.C. Bar Association. He formerly served as a U.S. Department of State Consular Officer with experience in visa processing at U.S. embassies abroad. He teaches classes on legal topics at the University of Klagenfurt and the Carinthia Technical Institute in Austria, and served as Editor-in-Chief of the Southern Illinois University Law Journal.

Debbie M. Schell, JD is an attorney and author who practices with the Law Offices of Kurt A. Wagner. She is a member of the American Immigration Lawyers Association (AILA) and the Immigration and Nationality Law Committee of the Chicago Bar Association. Her experience with immigration began early, when her mother immigrated to the United States from Jamaica and her father came from

Belize. She has edited legal forms books as well as works on the law of asylum. Her clients include refugees, as well as individuals and companies seeking help with immigration issues. In addition, she has extensive experience with human rights issues related to employment and housing.

Richard E. Schell, JD is an attorney, author, and serves of Counsel to the Law Offices of Kurt A. Wagner. He has extensive legal editing and researching experience with a major legal publisher and in the areas of international law, immigration law, and agricultural law. He studied international law at the University of Notre Dame in London. He is also a frequent writer and speaker on international legal topics and small business development.